The Lifelines of Love

PETER KUROWSKI

A Division of WINEPRESS PUBLISHING

Pleasant Word (a division of WinePress Publishing, PO Box 428, Enumclaw, WA 98022) functions only as book publisher. As such, the ultimate design, content, editorial accuracy, and views expressed or implied in this work are those of the author.

Printed in the United States of America

ISBN 13: 978-1-4141-0687-8
ISBN 10: 1-4141-0687-4
Library of Congress Catalog Card Number: 2006900710

In thanksgiving to God for our parents:

Edward and Anna Kurowski

Melvin and Betty Lau

TABLE OF CONTENTS

FOREWORD

Pastor Kurowski's exceptional writing skills came to my attention years ago when he took a Doctor of Ministry course that I offer on Creative Preaching. When I learned that he had prepared a manuscript on marriage, I asked him to permit me to critique it. Immediately, I recognized his manual to be eminently worthy of publication and encouraged the author to pursue the matter further.

The result is the book you are now about to enjoy, *The Lifelines of Love*. It is skillfully crafted. Everything—from its alliterating chapter titles to its balanced sentences, sharp antitheses, and attractive word plays—demonstrates careful, almost painstaking workmanship. The occasional quotations, besides demonstrating that Dr. Kurowski is well-read on the subject of marriage, are worth reading in their own right; they are consistently helpful, never pedantic or obtrusive.

Especially noteworthy is the fact that this manual avoids the pitfall of so many books on marriage—suggesting practical tips for marital success that ultimately prove to be impractical, because they have no solid foundation in the Gospel, which alone can empower happy and God-pleasing marriages. The word *lifelines* in the title sets the Gospel tone of the entire presentation. Nor is its

Gospel merely a code word; the Gospel is repeatedly spelled out in orthodox yet creative variety.

I am proud to recommend this book to Christian pastors, marriage counselors, marriage enrichment and encounter groups, Bible classes, youth groups, and other church organizations.

—Dr. Francis C. Rossow

SPECIAL THANKS

Two special words of thanks bubble forth. We thank Lois Wyse for permission to use her beautiful poem "Non-Stop" from the book, *Love Poems For the Very Married*. Also, we thank our artist, Jennifer Huecker, from Lone Elm, Missouri. Solely as a labor of love for Christ, Jennifer contributed her considerable talents to enhance *The Lifelines of Love*.

ACKNOWLEDGMENTS

This book could not have appeared without the help of "one hundred and one saints." At several junctures the book almost joined the swollen ranks of unpublished manuscripts. However, a word of encouragement, an open door, or the answer to prayer would drive me back to the computer keyboard. And here we are now with the third edition. God be praised!

Among my literary prodders were my caring professors of the Doctor of Ministry program of Concordia Seminary, St. Louis. With pastors' hearts and scholars' brains, they provided the "word fitly spoken" (Proverbs 25:11). However, the first inspiration came from loving laity who thirsted for a book on marriage that offered more than guidelines on marriage, but also *The Lifelines of Love.*

I wish to thank the saints who purchased copies for the first and second editions of *The Lifelines of Love.* Largely by word of mouth it keeps going. The excellent questions at the back of the book come from Pastor Todd Jerabek. They help to make *Lifelines* a good tool for premarital counseling and marriage retreats. It was Augustine who said the key to breaking the back of a challenging issue was to ask tough questions. We hope these questions will help the saints think through: "What does this mean?"

Finally, we pray again that this edition of *The Lifelines of Love* will help people see how Jesus leads us and feeds us. Especially, we pray that it points people to the marks of the Church—Word and Sacrament. By these marks and means, the Spirit enables us to run the good race by God's great grace as we behold the face of the Lord of life, Jesus Christ.

> *To this end may God be glorified,*
> *His redeemed edified,*
> *In the name of the Crucified,*
> *Risen Savior of sinners,*
> *Messiah Lord Jesus!*

Dr. Pastor Pete
January 1, 2006

FOUNDATION

I was conducting a late-night counseling session with newlyweds. John and Mary were scratching the seven-year itch by the seventh week of their marriage. The strands of commitment that held this marriage together were paper thin.

Strengthening the strands between John and Mary would not be easy. They dwelt far from the things of God. They almost never stepped foot into a house of God. The cover of their family Bible was protected with a thick layer of dust. Consequently, they severed themselves from the lifelines and guidelines of God's love. Nevertheless, in response to a plea from a relative of theirs and a friend of mine, I went to their home to work toward reconciliation.

It was about 10:30 P.M. when I arrived at their home to work out an eleventh-hour solution. As I sat down to speak with John and Mary, their red-shot eyes evinced a grim fatigue that said, "Let's hurry up and get this over with." How long the respirator of family pressure could keep alive their dying love could be measured in minutes, not days and weeks.

The Problem

I remember years ago reading a story about the famous boxer, Jersey Joe Walcott. After being knocked out by the great heavyweight champion Joe Louis, he was asked, "What happened?" Walcott's answer was straight, forward, and simple, "You can't do it, if you don't have it!"

Mary and John were in Jersey Joe's shoes. They simply "did not have it" to carry on the fight for their marriage. Lacking both the technique of how to love, as well as the tenacity to love, their marriage was about to go down for the ten count.

Mary and John needed new life in their marriage. Inhaling the noxious fumes of pride, exhaling in each other's face the halitosis of accusations, they needed the fresh air of God's love in Christ. Only the breath of the Spirit of God could resuscitate this marriage from otherwise death by divorce.

Men Are Snips and Snails and Puppy Dog Tails

After a brief prayer with the troubled couple, I asked them what they perceived to be the stress points of their marriage. It did not take long for them to vent their spleens. Mary led with her grievances:

"He daily calls his old girlfriends on the phone."

"He refuses to take care of his own child."

"He does not look for a job."

"He won't show me a bit of affection."
"He doesn't talk to me any more."

Women Are Sugar and Spice and Everything Nice

Mary's series of haymakers and left hooks solved her last outrage. She sparked John into talking to her! It was tough talk as he began to verbally counterpunch. "Moving like a butterfly and stinging like a bee," he went for the knockout:

"You are driving us to the poor house with your addiction to credit cards."

"You won't let me pursue my dream of becoming an entertainer."

"You are putting on weight like a sumo wrestler."

"You nag, nag, nag."

"You don't give me any space."

A Ministerial Maalox Moment

Quickly I had gone from a mediator to a referee. Inside I felt like screaming, "That's enough you two! Go to your respective corners. Let the 'fight' doctors attend to your wounds and we will call it a night." Instead, quietly pausing to pray for patience, masking my feelings during this Maalox moment, I politely said, "You have given me quite enough for us to discuss."

There was no mistaking this couple for Ward and June Cleaver. Actually, their behavior aped Mr. and Mrs. Meat Cleaver, dicing up each other with the cruel cuts of caustic comments. Moreover, each had the eye of an eagle when it came to the faults of the other; and both were as blind as moles when it came to their own shortcomings.

Where Love is Thin, Faults are Thick

Thomas Carlyle wrote, "The greatest of faults, I should say, is to be conscious of none." By Carlyle's standard, Mary and John were both unconscious. Both were oblivious to their own shortcomings.

Both were guilty of trying to rip planks out of the other's eyes when they had sequoia trunks in their own (Matthew 7:2-4).

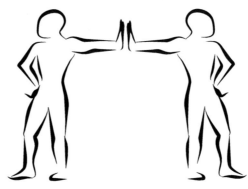

THE RELIGION OF SELF-JUSTIFICATION

The unnoticed log lodges readily into our eyes when the religion of self-justification worms its way into the shrine of our hearts. From almost the beginning of history, the religion of self-justification has led to a world of problems in general and marital misery in particular. Think about it. Was not this problem of John and Mary the same as that of "Pa" Adam and "Ma" Eve in the Garden, when the first marital clash took place? (Genesis 3:1-13).

THE FIRST FIGHT

Go back to the Garden of Eden, to the time when Adam and Eve ate the forbidden fruit (Genesis 2:17), thereby telling God to "go fly a kite!" Before this tragic moment in time, there had been perfect horizontal harmony between each other and heavenly vertical harmony with God. As a couple they had had no fights, no misunderstandings, and no power plays. However, their arrogant ascent to be equal with God backfired, becoming a devilish descent to evil. Their power play needled into their veins the deadly "me first" virus known as sin. The "me first" poison of their actions turned the loving couple into a warring couple. Worse yet, by eating the forbidden fruit, they gave birth among humanity to the destructive spirit of self-justification.

The Blame Game

When God confronted Adam with his sin, all the man of clay could do was to blame others. Justifying his actions, Adam said, "God, the woman You gave me—*she* gave me some fruit from the tree and I ate it" (Genesis 3:12). Nice guy. In one sentence he absolves himself by blaming both God and Eve for his predicament. For the over 900 years Adam walked this earth, he had to try to live down this most infamous of accusations (Genesis 5:4).

Eve—a bit more subtle, but just as spiritually blind—also tried to shift the blame. Her self-justifying response was, "The serpent hoodwinked me, and I ate" (Genesis 3:13). Together, she and Adam transferred this perverse habit of self-justification, original sin, to John and Mary, as well as all of humanity.

Will Rogers once said that the history of America could be divided into three stages, "the passing of the buffalo, the passing of the American Indian, and the passing of the buck." "Passing the buck," or "*self-justification*," is the native path of natural man. Unless checked by God's Law and changed by the Gospel, it leads to marital misery and eternal disaster.

The Malady – The Cure

Many a marriage counselor will tell you that self-justification is the root of all matrimonial woes. You won't get anywhere until this spiritual disease is diagnosed and continuously treated. And what is the remedy to this malady? The cure of man's self-justification is God's justification!

Without using justification jargon, I sought to set forth in simple terms this teaching to John and Mary. As a Lutheran pastor, I believe that the teaching is not only the bedrock belief on which the Church stands or falls, but it is also love's lifeline to couples. It is this teaching that creates faith and love in human hearts. The knowledge that God declares sinners "saints" for the sake of His dear Son who died for them is the greatest declaration in history. It is this Magna Carta of forgiveness and love that breaks the stranglehold of sin and frees people from the perverse spirit of self-justification.

However, before John and Mary could appreciate this Good News, they needed to hear a word of bad news. For the Good News that God, for Jesus' sake, declares not guilty the ungodly (Romans 4:5) is water off a duck's back to a person who has no sense of sin. John and Mary needed to take a close look into the mirror of God's Law (Romans 3:20). If they were honest, they would by the light of the Law see that a number of the things they were doing as husband and wife were loveless—offensive to each other and to God.

THE LAW

Gently but firmly, I told John that it was neither a loving thing nor a God-pleasing act to be talking with former girlfriends on the phone. He needed to confess this as sin before God and put his communication skills to work in his marriage. I told him that it was also wrong for him to neglect his son and to look half-heartedly for work, since his attitude of sloth and indolence was spreading like gangrene into other aspects of his life.

Mary also heard the Law. I explained to her that she needed to confess to God her sin of worshiping credit cards and trying to find joy in the things of this world over the things of God. To her credit, she readily admitted that she had gone way overboard with her plastic and would try to turn over a new leaf. She also agreed that her nagging needed to give way to a pattern of speaking the truth in love.

THE GOSPEL

Both Mary and John were assured that Jesus Christ, the holy Son of God, had in love already paid for these sins by His death on the cross. In addition, they heard what Jesus could do for them *now* through His Church and the grace-giving channels of love: Word and Sacrament. He that loved them and gave His life for them was eager as Risen Lord to give them power from on high: power for here below. The Church, I informed them, was the retreat center to hear the renewing message of God's love, which in turn creates within us the love needed for marriage.

WHY SOME, NOT OTHERS?

With the hand of faith, Mary gave every evidence of laying hold of this Good News of a Savior who loved her and died for her and could bring help for her troubled marriage. John, on the other hand, sat emotionless on his island chair, giving little evidence that he was guilty of any self-justification and in need of the help that comes from Jesus Christ through the Church. My fear was that the similar measure of the Law, which revealed to Mary a sense of her sin and her need for Jesus, had not jarred John out of his smug, self-justifying ways.

Dwight Moody once said, "God sends no one away empty except those who are full of themselves." In a few moments, I would find out if John had laid hold of what I sensed Mary now believed, the Good News of God's love in Jesus Christ. With the lateness of the hour at hand, with the law of diminishing returns about to strike the midnight hour, it was time to close the session.

"John and Mary," I asked, "can you please tell me what or who is the key to your marriage?" The silent husband remained mute. Mary had given her husband first opportunity to speak, but he only hung his head. After a pause that seemed like hours, Mary answered, "Jesus Christ."

My heart inwardly sang when I heard the evening air fill with these beautiful words. "Your answer is correct, Mary! Would you answer me another question?" "I'll try," she said. "How can Jesus give you and John strength and grace to pull together and work together?" Again she answered very well, "Through the Church, through those spiritual lifelines you call the means of grace: Word and Sacrament."

As I heard Mary's two-fold, heaven-born confession, part of me was elated while part of me was downcast. The latter mood sprang from her listless husband. Theirs was a marriage where only one of the two wanted Jesus to transform it through His powerful means of grace. Filled with the self-satisfaction of the devil's food, John wanted none of the Bread of Life that Jesus imparts.

The bitter-sweet story of John and Mary illustrates that the grace of God needed to transfigure disfigured relationships can be rejected. Though the grace of God is a never-failing source of renewal, it can be resisted and refused. Unfortunately, John turned down the invitation to feed from the Bread of Life in favor of eating the bread of sorrows. He was not interested in hearing about either the guidelines of love (Law) or the lifelines of love (Gospel). Ultimately, his unbelief would lead to the death of his and Mary's marriage.

Was Samuel Johnson Right?

Samuel Johnson once said, "Men do not need to be informed of something new, as to be reminded of what they know." There is much truth to this. On the other hand, in our age when most people are quite confused and ignorant as to what love really is and how God imparts it, Johnson's statement appears to be overly optimistic.

Beyond Guidelines

In recent years, scores of books on marriage have been turned out to give guidance to couples as to how to work together and live together. Most of them, be they secular or sacred, offer plenty of sound guidelines for good marriages. Frankly, except for a few promiscuous pens, many secular writers offer advice on par with Christian authors. In reality, the common note of the good "how to" books on marriage is the Law of God.

This is all fine and good where couples have a high degree of motivation to make their marriage work. But what happens when the oomph and energy to carry out the instructions of the good "how to" books are lacking? How does one find strength to follow the 200 rules, 250 principles, 100 maxims, 150 steps, and 301 exercises to have a marriage that is a foretaste of heaven rather than a foretaste of hell?

Here is the problem. Though the Law of God is good (1 Timothy 1:8), the Old Adam is bad. Many of the authors of books on marriage tend to overlook the long roots of sin. They forget the fact that this side of heaven the Old Adam has set up permanent squatter rights in our heart. Even after coming to faith in Jesus, our sinful flesh still wants to run life on its own terms (Romans 8:17). It wants nothing to do with the Law of God despite the fact that keeping the Law is the good life (Galatians 5:22).

LAW APPROACH = PALL RESULTS

The problem is not made easier by the Law, for it tells us what to do, but does not help us do it. On top of that, when we fail to keep the Law, it "stirs up sin" (Romans 7:5) and "reveals to us our sin" (Romans 3:20). If our diet is only Law, or primarily Law, then we will continuously feel wretched-minded (Romans 7:24). Thus, if marriage books are no more than "how to" documents and guideline givers, then by the sheer weight of the Law they will create spiritual fatigue, not faith; guilt, not good impulses; heavy hearts, not absolved consciences.

This is not an attack on good "how to" books. They are necessary and are salutary whenever one listens to that little inner voice box called the conscience. Yet marriage books need to not only address the guidelines of love, but also offer the lifelines of love.

OLD STORY, NEW TWIST

Understanding what are the lifelines of love *and* how God communicates to us are of utmost importance. An apocryphal story on lifelines underscores this point. A certain woman was caught in a nasty storm where rain was coming down by buckets and barrels. As the water began to rise and the streets began to flood, a jacked-up four-wheeler jeep drove up to her house. A friend from the jeep called out, "Come with me and let me drive you to higher ground." The woman responded, "No thanks, I have prayed to the Lord and He will rescue me."

Soon the waters had risen several feet. The woman remained undaunted. A civil defense boat made its way to her home. The man in the boat beckoned her to come aboard and vacate her home before the waters would overtake her. She replied, "No thank you, I have prayed to the Lord and He will rescue me."

The heavy rains continued. The waters rose steadily. Now the woman found herself in her upstairs bedroom as the first floor was completely submerged. Hearing the sound of a helicopter, she went to the window and opened it. A rescue unit shouted to her to lay hold of the lifeline and they would pull her aboard. She yelled to them, "No thank you, I have prayed to the Lord and He will rescue me."

An hour later the misguided woman drowned.

Arriving in heaven, she met St. Peter at the pearly gates. Irritated, she asked, "Why didn't the Lord rescue me when I called upon Him?" Checking his records St. Peter said, "It states here that the Lord sent three different crews to rescue you and you refused all three!"

How God's Grace Comes to Us

The living God, as one pastor used to say, "does not bushwhack people in blind alleys." He comes to us by means He has ordained. He uses certain lifelines as a conduit for His mercy, grace, and love to us.

What are these lifelines of love? What are the means by which Jesus distributes and dispenses His Holy Spirit and the love of God? How does Jesus grant to couples the "oomph" and *energy* to "love one another," "to be kind to one another," "to forgive one another," and "to serve one another"? After all, the Law commands us to do all of these good things for building strong marriages.

The Problem of the Gap

In recent years, Professor Kurt Marquart has answered this critical question effectively under the heading of "The Problem of the Gap." The "Problem of the Gap" is this. How can we be in touch with Jesus today in the 1990's? How does the Risen Lord Jesus of

THE LIFELINES OF LOVE

circa 33 A.D. become a resurrection reality for Christian couples some 1,900 years later?

The Bible answers these questions beautifully and clearly. The space-time gap can be bridged only from God's side and not ours. In other words, because we cannot go back to Calvary, the benefits of Calvary and the open tomb must come to us.

According to scripture, Jesus comes to us and bestows grace upon us in vehicles and vessels that He has set up and set forth. He comes to us through the Gospel Word of Holy Baptism, the Lord's Supper, Holy Absolution, and in the purely-preached Gospel. In this four-fold way, His four-fold love (Ephesians 3:18) tabernacles among us. This is how the Savior of sinners and marriages bridges the gap, bringing to us *today* the benefits of Good Friday and Easter Sunday.

GOD'S WAYS ARE NOT OUR WAYS

Throughout the Bible, we see God coming to men and women in unexpected ways. The world did not expect the Son of God to be born in lowly Bethlehem. Swaddling clothes, rather than royal robes, would not have been the way we would have dressed the Messiah. Being born of a poor Jewish family in a backwater province, rather than of a Caesar under a regal Roman roof, is such an odd way for God to make personal contact.

Yet this is the way Christ chose to come into the world. Even more shocking is God's method of rescuing us from sin and eternal death. Human minds often stumble over the "foolish" way (1 Corinthians 1:23) in which God came to rescue sinners—the cross. The Old Testament prophecy of "cursed is he who dies on a tree" (Deuteronomy 21:22-23) underscores the stunning nature of His rescue mission. With this instrument of death, God would bring about life. By this means God would unexpectedly cross up the Devil and cross out our sin, making full atonement for the sin of the world (1 John 2:2).

God Still Comes to Us in Unexpected Fashion

Today He still comes to us in unexpected fashion. The cruses that carry the benefits from the cross are not visionary vessels but again simple acts: Baptism, the Lord's Supper, Holy Absolution, and the preaching of the Gospel. In hiddenness, in humility, and through Word and Sacrament, we see the marks of the Church and have the means by which the Church is created and sustained. Similarly we have, in these means, marks that are the contact points by which the Lord of the Church creates love and touches lives.

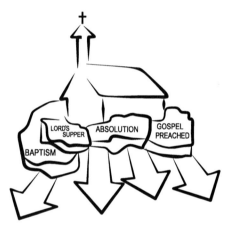

Where do you see and find the living God? Look for the marks of Christ's Church, the means of Grace! John Madden, the former football coach and current television commentator, tells an interesting story about Ray Wersching, a field goal kicker for the San Francisco '49ers. Wersching has an interesting technique when he lines up to attempt a field goal. He *never* looks at the goal posts. The holder has to tell him if a kick is successful.

"But how do you aim," Madden once asked him, "if you don't look at the goal posts?"

"I just look at the hash marks," replied Wersching. "They tell me all I have to know."

Madden went on to say that Wersching was right. The hash marks, those chalked lines about 23 yards inside each sideline on a football field, are 18-1/2 feet apart, the same width as the goal posts. These hash marks are the marks that Wersching looks at to see the goal clearly.

"The farther away you are, the narrower the goal posts look," Ray Wersching explains, "but the hash marks always look wide!"

THE HASH MARKS OF THE CHURCH

The hash marks of the Church and the lifelines of love by which we see the living God are the doctrine of justification and the means of grace. In moving away from a focus on either of these, numerous dangers to marriage increase. Where these teachings hover at the center of one's life, the lifelines of love lift couples up, bringing God's grace to His children. As a pastor, I have noticed the tragedy that comes when couples have something other than Jesus and His means of grace as the center of their focus. It might be money, corporate success, fame, personal appearance, control over one's mate, sex, or any number of golden calves. These props may serve well as long as the storms of life are mild and moderate, but they won't provide what is needed to withstand the more turbulent trials and temptations that threaten marriage.

DON'T TURN YOUR SPOUSE INTO AN ASHERAH POLE (1 KINGS 14:23)

How often couples waltz into marriage with the Cinderella and Prince Charming syndrome. They think that if they just find the right person they will live happily ever after. That is a lot of pressure to put on the shoulders of a finite, fallen, human being. No matter how good and capable one's spouse is, he or she cannot be the source of ultimate happiness and pleasure. We must remember that the wedding vows are "I do," not "Idol!"

One book on marriage I read a long time ago had an intriguing title: *Happy Though Married*. While there is a note of tragedy in the title, it can serve to remind us that the deepest joy in life comes not from one's mate but one's Master, Jesus Christ—and that joy descends to us through Word and Sacrament. Just as air and food are needed for the body, Word and Sacrament are needed to sustain faith and love within the marriage. Through these means God supplies to married couples an enduring, endearing love.

A TRULY EVANGELICAL EMPHASIS

A fellow co-worker in Christ once told me, "A person can read scores of how-to books on marriage, but without the lifeblood of Word and Sacrament, they won't provide the real help a Christian couple needs." This saint was not denigrating "how-to" books, but requesting a marriage book holding high both the *lifelines* of love with the *guidelines* of love. Both are needed. The first provides the power to love; the second provides the pattern for love.

FORGIVENESS

It was Dr. Leslie Weatherhead who wrote, "The forgiveness of God, in my opinion, is the most powerful and therapeutic idea in the world." I agree. It is this lifeline and guideline that comes to us from the living God—the living God Who delights in forgiving us because of what His Son did for us!

It was the Son of the living God, Jesus Christ, who turned aside the holy wrath of God. Instead of punishment for our sins, we received pardon. Jesus did this by serving as a lightening rod for God's just anger, bringing us instead the electricity of God's forgiveness.

Through the conduits of Word and Sacrament, the gift of forgiveness comes to us from God. As it does, it creates faith and love, the two bands that bond couples together!

Billy Graham Cites Key to a Good Marriage

Dr. Billy Graham applied the words of Dr. Weatherhead to holy matrimony when he said, "The key to a good marriage is two good forgivers." There is no finer fuel for high-octane marriages than forgiveness of sins. It provides power for love. It is the driving force behind needed, ongoing reconciliation.

Dr. Martin Luther once remarked, "The forgiveness of sins is the chief part of Christian teaching and I am completely steeped in, and saturated with, the article of the forgiveness of sins." You know, Luther was married. Do you think this man steeped in the teaching of forgiveness was a pretty good hubby?

E. Jane Mall's delightful little book, *Kitty My Rib*, the beloved name Luther gave his mate, gives fascinating insights into the very good marriage of Martin Luther and Katherine von Bora.

The Glue of a Good Marriage

At the center of their marriage was the bringer of forgiveness of sins, Jesus Christ. It was this gift, forgiveness of sins, which enabled two strong-willed and different personalities, Martin and Katherine, to forgive one another, and with that forgiveness, to grow in holy love. It was this gift that taught Luther how to validate his wife. Of his domestic engineer, he said, "My Katie is in all things so obliging and pleasing to me that I would not exchange my poverty for the riches of Croesus."

Luther's validation engendered appreciation. Shortly after his death, Katherine said of Luther, "Who would not be sorrowful and mourn for so noble a man as was my dear lord, who served not only one city or a single land, but the whole world? This dear and precious man." Evidently, forgiving and loving went hand in hand.

Forgiveness of sins ranks as both our greatest gift and greatest resource. With this gift, God makes enemies friends and good friends stronger friends. Through this gift, God brought about a change between Himself and the world with what is known as "the happy exchange."

The Happy Exchange!

"The happy exchange" involved God sending His Son to suffer hell that we might have heaven, being forsaken that we might be forgiven, and suffering an eternal death that we might have eternal life. Jesus brought about this "happy exchange" by what He endured on a cross for six hours on Good Friday and what He accomplished by His perfect life of thirty-three years. Never forget that He did these things for us! He brought about a reconciliation that has power not only to save us from sin, but also to help us overcome what otherwise might be labeled "irreconcilable differences." St. Paul describes this Good News: "But God has done it all. When we were His enemies, through Christ He made us His friends and gave us the work of making friends of enemies" (2 Corinthians 5:18).

"The Happy Exchange" Produces Happy Marriages

Just as the life and death of Christ changed the relationship of the whole world before God, it can change, for the better, relationships between spouses. The same God Who "in Christ reconciled the world to Himself by not counting their sins against them" (2 Corinthians 5:19) also rescues marriages. In fact, the more couples know through faith that "God is for them," the more they can truly be for each other. It is God's unconditional love and forgiveness that creates the faith and love so desperately needed by beleaguered couples.

A Real-life Drama

Never was this truth expressed to me more poignantly than in a real-life drama that enlisted my services. It began with a phone call from a desperate, grief-stricken husband. The quivering voice of Frank informed me that his spouse was sexually involved with another man. My ears listened more than my mouth moved. His initial need was a friend to listen.

Eventually, Frank asked me to come to his home later that day. He planned to confront his wife, Kim, with the evidence of her infidelity. Fearing that his anger might lead him to folly, he requested that I come and serve as a go-between. His trembling request was followed by my shaky, "Certainly."

A FAMILIAR PATTERN

Neither Kim nor Frank had "darkened the door" of the church for several months. Absence from the lifelines of love contributed to the abandonment of the guidelines of love. Adultery followed idolatry. Love had given way to lust.

Following the phone call with Frank, all kinds of questions began to explode in my mind. Would Kim be smug or sorry when confronted with the evidence? Did Frank drive Kim into this Bermuda-triangle relationship by unloving and uncaring acts? Would there be a violent war with words? If she was sorry, would Frank forgive her? What Word of God would I apply to this modern-day rerun of David and Bathsheba?

THE DOMINANT NOTE

I felt for both Kim and Frank. They loved their children and were pro-family. Frank, though a good man among men, was given toward making the Law the dominant note in their marriage. Accusation rather than validation was his style. For every good and kind word to build up Kim, he doled out four words to break her down.

Experts tell us that it takes four good words to cancel every cruel remark we dish out toward others. Frank had the whole formula backward. He was the accusative case in action. Added to this, he dispensed the Law in a lawless manner—harshly and severely.

GREASING THE SLOPES

One sure way to grease the slopes for one's spouse to slide into another person's arms (and bed) is to harp and carp at them all the time. This is the fertilizer the devil and his filthy crew use to make the marital grass look greener elsewhere.

Scripture encourages the dominant note of marriages to be one of nurturing and nourishing (Ephesians 5:29), not one of criticism and condemnation. When criticism must be dispensed, gentleness and humility are the watchwords (Galatians 6:1).

Here is a good rule of thumb. Treat the faults of others as graciously as you treat your own. Thomas a' Kempis has said, "He that well and rightly considers his own works, will find little cause to judge harshly of another." When, through the Law, we see the enormity of our sin, and through the Gospel see the surpassing love of Christ's forgiveness, we receive grace to treat others graciously.

SURPRISE!

The afternoon drive to Frank's house to meet with a traumatized husband and a soon-to-be-traumatized wife went all too quickly. Before I knew it, I was walking up to the front door of Kim' and Frank's home. To my surprise it was open.

Instincts told me to ignore the doorbell and enter. As I stepped into the foyer, the sobbing and weeping of an emotionally disheveled couple drew me further. Moving into the next room, a startling sight caught my eyes. Frank had his arms around Kim. No, he was not hurting nor harming her, but holding her, tenderly and sensitively.

On my way over to their home, I had prepared several short speeches for possible scripts. However, no speeches were prepared for this scenario. This blessed dilemma had my tongue tied in knots.

Kim and Frank finally sensed my presence. Noticing the astonished look on my face, Frank spoke: "Pastor, I am sorry I did not wait for you to get here. I just could not wait. I decided to confront Kim with the news before you came."

"That's ... that's okay," I sputtered.

THE AWESOME POWER OF ABSOLUTION

Pausing for a few moments, Frank proceeded to explain what had happened. With a lump in his throat and tears in his eyes, he spoke humbly from the heart, "I told Kim that if Jesus could forgive me *all* my sins, I could forgive her of this!"

Frank's awesome words of absolution were words sent from heaven. They stunned me. They broke down Kim's defenses. They melted her heart and moved mine. Spoken sincerely and simply, Frank's words had a Damascus Road effect upon Kim. The word of forgiveness in Christ's name had turned mourning into a new morning. Forgiveness planted faith, and from faith hope blossomed.

Frank allowed me to have a few minutes alone with Kim. He sensed that she needed to have a few private moments to speak to her pastor. After brief counsel with Kim, I asked Frank to join her for a moment of prayer and the benediction. Then I urged them, by the mercies of Christ, to attend church the following Sunday. There they would find added help and healing in God's forgiveness to begin putting the past behind them and moving ahead with God's grace.

Returning to my car, I felt like pinching myself to make sure that what I had witnessed was real and not some kind of dream. It was not a dream. It was a miracle.

It was a miracle born as a result of Frank's remarkable and loving confession—a confession born not of flesh and blood, but of the Spirit of God through the forgiveness that Christ brings.

THE MIRROR OF THE LAW

Through the mirror of the Law, the Holy Spirit had enabled Frank to recognize his own sin and how it contributed to driving Kim into another person's arms. Evidently, from the time Frank and I had ended our phone conversation, he had done a lot of soul searching. Through the Word, the Spirit had made him "poor in spirit" that he might "mourn" over his sin and in "meekness" inherit a bit of the earth (Matthew 5:3-5).

Through the mirror to God's heart, the cross, the Holy Spirit enlightened Frank to see the greatness of Christ's love and the gift of love—forgiveness. This gift became the cornerstone of his confession. On this cornerstone, he found footing to stand tall and pardon Kim of her sin, as well as admit to Kim his sin.

THE MOVEMENT OF LOVE

Note well the progression of the confession. It began with God's love in Christ. It moved to the gift of forgiveness of sins. From there faith followed, and a wondrous word of absolution came forth. The hymn writer puts it nicely:

"Love to the loveless shown that they might lovely be."
(Hymn 91, verse 1, *Lutheran Worship*)

37

It was the forgiveness of Christ that first thawed Frank's heart and then defrosted Kim's soul. By grace through faith in Christ, forgiveness had come to this hurting household. By God's grace the marriage of Kim and Frank was saved. The doctrine of justification, which is really the doctrine of forgiveness, had rescued, resurrected, and restored another relationship.

Follow-up

Later, I met with Kim and Frank to offer added support. Ongoing encouragement in a fallen world is always necessary. The Good News of forgiveness must be spoken to our assurance-needing hearts all the time. Everyday, we need to have our minds massaged by the message that God's forgiveness in Christ is free and full. No sin is too large, no sins are too many, and no conditions must be met to usher in the forgiveness of God through Jesus Christ.

It was this last point where Kim and Frank were struggling and stumbling days later, when they came to my office. Unwittingly, they were allowing a work they thought they must do to obscure the great work Christ had done. They needed to understand the crucial distinction between forgiving and forgetting.

Granted, good forgivers tend to be good forgetters. By not dwelling on the past, they can move forward. They don't seek, as one veteran pastor once told me, "to re-open old cow pies." That is a situation where both parties become losers!

Forgiving Equals Forgetting???

Early in one of the follow-up sessions, Kim and Frank expressed the frustration they carried because they were unable to "forget" the affair. A zillion cues would wing it to the forefront of their minds. Harboring the notion that "failure to forget is just another excuse to fail to forgive," they were miserable.

I cringe when literature implies that, in order to forgive someone, you must delete from your brain all data relating to the past offense that made you its target. A sort of spiritual shock therapy.

This counsel, brought to you by Job's friends, advises that if you have not forgotten, then you have not forgiven.

CORRECT GOSPEL TEACHING

Correct gospel teaching does two things. It gives God glory and brings poor sinners comfort. The equation that forgiving means mental forgetting does neither, for it fails to properly divide Law and Gospel.

Let's examine this thesis. Is it true that forgiveness and forgetfulness are synonymous buddies? Does anyone really think that Kim and Frank could ever erase the knowledge of this affair from their minds? Short of sheer memory loss, the awareness of the affair could not be edited out of their craniums. The knowledge of the affair would likely go with them to the grave.

UNMASKING LEGALISM

At stake here is the idea that forgiveness is contingent upon our forgetfulness. Examining this under the microscope of God's Word, we see the germ of legalism. "Legalism" means "salvation by works." Speaking about "salvation by works," scripture says it just doesn't work! We are saved by grace alone, Jesus alone, faith alone (Ephesians 2:8, 9; Galatians 3:10; Acts 16:31).

To assert that to forgive means to forget is to base forgiveness not only on what Jesus has done, but also on what we must do; namely, remove mental recollections from our mind. Beloved, "forgetting" is not a requirement for forgiveness. Forgiveness is a purely 100 percent gift (Romans 4:24)! No conditions. It's free! Free! Free! Free!

A CLOSER LOOK AT SCRIPTURE

One suspects that this dangerous notion, that forgiveness entails forgetfulness, springs from the misreading of certain passages in scripture. For example, the Bible does say that God will "no longer remember sins" (Jeremiah 31:34). Interpreted apart from the rest of scripture, one could conclude that if God does not remember sins, then we should not remember them either. Such a conclusion attacks the very nature and promises of God.

Concerning the nature of God, the Bible states that He knows *all* things (Psalms 139:1-4). To teach that God is prone to a divine lapse in memory is more than precarious. Even after His bodily resurrection from the dead, Jesus cognitively *remembered* Peter's sinful threefold denial (John 21:15-17), despite forgiving Him (John 20:22-23; 2 Corinthians 5:19).

Key Question

How then do we line up the verse of scripture that says of God, "...and their sin I will remember no more" (Jeremiah 31:34) with other portions of scripture that testify God is all-knowing (Psalms 139:1-4; John 21:17)? We line it up by obtaining a proper understanding of the meaning of the Hebrew word for "remember," *zachar*.

In matters pertaining to God's no longer remembering sin, *zachar* does not mean God is intellectually forgetful, but that He *will not get even*. He will not get even, because He *got even* when He made His Son, Jesus, the atonement price for our sin, and the sin of the world (1 John 2:1). In other words, He *forgot* our sins when He *remembered* that they were nailed on the cross.

Forgiveness Applied

Once Kim and Frank understood that no longer remembering sins was a matter of *not getting even,* rather than *forgetting,* they could breathe easier and move ahead without the misplaced weight of the Law on their backs. Through all of this they learned that to forgive means that by the grace of God, one will strive *not* to bring up the past sins of others.

For good marriages, the good riddance of the score-keeper syndrome is essential. It keeps the lines of communication open.

It allows old wounds time to be healed. It is also the way of love. In describing the *not getting even* side of love, St. Paul wrote: "Love has good manners and does not pursue selfish advantage. It is not touchy. *It does not keep account of evil,* or gloat over the wickedness of other people" (1 Corinthians 13:5-7 PHILLIPS).

FORGIVENESS AND FORBEARANCE

Intimately related to the concept of forgiveness, and equally needed in Christian marriage, is the Gospel-given quality known as forbearance. Spouses need to for*bear* with one another because, at times, they can really be un*bear*able. In discussing the "bond of peace" between and among Christians, St. Paul enjoins them to live a life "with all humility and gentleness, with patience, showing *forbearance* to one another in love" (Ephesians 4:2 NAS).

Forgiveness and forbearance go hand in hand. The first trait deals with not seeking to get even with someone who has wronged us. The latter virtue is the ability to put up with an individual's short-comings and peculiarities.

Face it—after the wedding vows, new faults have a way of surfacing. Everything from who controls the thermostat to how the socks are folded can become irritants that call for forbearance. Needed is no-fault insurance. Mark Twain was right when he said, "Love is blind, but marriage is a good optometrist." No wonder St. Paul exhorted Ephesians couples to "generously make allowances for each other because you love each other" (Ephesians 4:2 PHILLIPS).

I know my mate must put up with plenty of my faults. Often, when Jan talks to me, I am wrapped up in a pastoral concern and she must call out repeatedly, "Earth to Peter, earth to Peter." After 20 years of marriage, I still have the lunkhead habit of putting empty water bottles or milk cartons in the refrigerator. The comedian Seinfeld had me pegged when he said that most "men don't watch television, they just wonder what is on the other channels."

A number of writers around the world and from different eras have recognized the need for forbearance. A French proverb states that "a good husband should be deaf and a good wife blind." Various sages from Martin Luther to Ben Franklin have quipped to the effect, "Before marriage keep both eyes open; after marriage keep only one eye open!"

No Perfect Spouses

All these observations teach the need for forbearance, as well as the need to remember that there are no perfect spouses. If a person is expecting perfection or near perfection from their spouse, then one has a superficial view of sin—one's own, as well as that of one's spouse. Only one Person qualified as a perfect spouse, and He got away! He was Jesus (2 Corinthians 5:21). By divine plan He remained single in order that He might single-mindedly go to the cross to provide the forgiveness and love needed to hold together marriages.

There are no utopian unions of man and woman. To expect a perfect marriage is to invite fractured fairy tales. Because each person in the marriage is, as the ancient liturgy sets forth, "a poor miserable sinner," a wellspring of forbearance is always needed.

Reality Check

Forbearance and forgiveness grow wherever God's Word of Law and Gospel guide and gear hearts and homes. Regular reading of God's Word reduces fault-finding in the following manner. If the sin-exposing Law of God is read correctly, then we will see that we, ourselves, have committed an astronomical number of sins (Matthew 18:23). Such a realization will keep an honest and humble person from saddling the high horse of pride and plowing over his spouse. John Ruskin has said, "Pride is at the bottom of all great mistakes."

Augustus Toplady, the author of "Rock of Ages," once estimated that by the time a person reaches the age of 20, they have committed a whopping 630,000,000 sins against God. Actually, it is impossible to keep a tally of sin, for as Luther says, "We sin in all we do!" When one considers that all sin is as serious as the one it offends, and that it is always "spitting in God's face" (Numbers 12:14), sin is never a minor matter.

Once I asked one of my eighth-grade catechetical students, "How often do you think that God forgives us?" Dawn's answer was...

GOOGOLPLEXES!

"Googolplexes!" Her answer was terrific on two accounts. One, the word "googolplex" describes well the enormity of our sin, for googolplex is a term which signifies 1 with 100 zeroes behind it. Two, in the dictionary the word "googolplexes" comes just before the word "gospel." The Gospel is the Good News that, though we sin against God "googolplexes" of times, He declares us, because of His dear Son, "not guilty," "forgiven," and "justified" (Romans 4:5).

While it is the Law of God that can knock a rough rider off his or her high horse, it is the Gospel that enables us to ride into the Holy City on a donkey with humility and gentleness (Matthew 21:2-5). In light of the Good News that for Jesus' sake God drives away sin "as far as the east is from the west" (Psalms 103:12), Christian couples find grace to forgive and forbear. Through the Gospel, couples can find strength to (like God) put sin behind their back (Isaiah 38:17).

A LOOK AT LUKE

Intimately connected to forgiveness is love. We see this in the story of Jesus and the sinful woman (Luke 7:36-50). Here Jesus declares a woman with a notorious past forgiven! By freely forgiving her, He places her in a right relationship with God (justification).

This Good News made her a new creature. Full of joy and love, she served the Savior with gladness. All of this moved Jesus to say of her, "That is why I tell you that her many sins have been

43

forgiven—as a result, she loved much. But he who has little for-given, loves little" (Free Translation, Luke 7:47). In short, where the appreciation of forgiveness of sin is Tom Thumb-like, love will be Lilliputian-like.

The Wide-ranging Dimensions of Forgiveness

The wide-ranging dimensions of forgiveness of sins—a gift from God which creates faith and love—affirm the power of this gift that resurrected Frank and Kim's marriage from the ash heap. It is a gift from Christ, through the Church, that can renew any marriage. Behind this awesome gift stands the towering cross on which the Lord of love, Jesus Christ, was crucified for the sins of the world (John 1:29).

The impulses married couples need for truly loving each other find their origin in the gift of "forgiveness of sins." It is not a gift given in isolation. Connected to it are *all* the gifts of heaven: God's grace, the Holy Spirit, Christ's merits, justification, life, reconcili-ation, and salvation.

Since the treasures of heaven are linked to this grand gift, for-giveness of sins, how vital it is that we are embraced by it continually and not sporadically. So that the love in our marriage might not dry up but well up, we need to recall how God dispenses this gift. To this end, the continuing significance of our baptism should not be overlooked. Many Christians forget, says Luther, "Baptism is in force all through life, even until death, yes ... even to the Last Day."

Daily Repentance Stirs
the Mighty Waters of Repentance

Through daily repentance, confession of our sins, and rejoicing in the gift of forgiveness of sins, the Holy Spirit stirs the waters of our baptism. As He stirs the waters through daily repentance, He drowns the Old Adam and brings to the surface our New Adam. It is the New Adam, the creature of love, who daily rises to build the marriage (Ephesians 4:22-32).

Beneath the keyboard of my computer are the words of Luther's Morning and Evening prayers. These prayers of repentance prod me to see my constant need to repent! Through repentance the Spirit stirs the waters of Holy Baptism with God's "yes" in Jesus, Who accepts the sinner!

When Luther declared in the first of his Ninety-five Theses that "the whole life of the Christian was to be a continual repentance," this was beautiful baptism language. It was a call to that blessed daily death called "Baptism." In Baptism we are brought into union with Christ (Romans 6:3). It is this union which can feed the marriage union. By daily repentance of our sins, we stake to the cross the arch enemy of any marriage, our sinful nature.

TROUBLED MARRIAGES – LITTLE REPENTANCE

Over the years I have observed that troubled marriages invariably are short on apologies and weak in the realm of personal repentance. Hard-to-live-with spouses find it extra hard to apologize to their partners, because they are not in the healthy habit of apologizing to God. It is too bad that Hollywood makes matters worse by dispensing sonic-debris statements such as, "Love means that you never have to say you're sorry!" That may apply to Jesus, but it certainly does not apply to us sinners.

REPENTANCE: GREAT GOSPEL GIFT

Repentance is the great Gospel gift (Acts 11:18). God desires His children to use it rigorously around the clock. The apostle John writes, "The blood of Jesus Christ constantly cleanses us from all sin" (1 John 1:7). Like a non-stopping windshield wiper blade at work, God's grace perpetually wipes away our sins. For Jesus' sake, God washes away all our zillions of sins. Sins of commission and omission receive remission continually. In fact, the more couples grow in faith in Jesus, they realize more keenly the enormity of their sin, even as they manifest the marriage-strengthening fruit of the Spirit (Galatians 5:22-23).

Repentance—God's gift—is the lift that every marriage needs for deep, deep love (Acts 11:18). This gift God grants through the justification juice of His unconditional love (Romans 4:5; 5:6). This juice comes from the Divine Vine (John 15) through the water of Baptism (Acts 2:38; Titus 3:4-7). In turn it gives us strength to nourish as well as flourish.

Repentance, fired by the message of the cross and fueled through the lifelines of love, breaks the grip of self-destructive patterns. An effective element of repentance is public confession, as well as private confession of *particular* sins (John 20:21-23; Mark 9:24; Psalms 73; James 5:16). Spiritual laser surgery through enumerating our sins before God cleans out the nooks and corners of our conscience. Often when saints come to their pastor for private confession and absolution, they have this epiphany. They say something like, "Pastor, I knew I was forgiven before. Now I really know I am forgiven." Through private confession and absolution Jesus breathes upon God's children not only added assurance, but added strength and added love.

There is an old saying that good habits are easy to live with and hard to develop; bad habits, on the other hand, are easy to develop but hard to live with. Cultivating the gift of repentance in public confession, in private confession, and in a life-long attitude connected with a life-long study of the Word, is a mighty outstanding holy habit to cultivate. Repentance, the work of the Holy Spirit through the means of grace, continually gives us the strength to draw from Christ's love. And Christ's love to us is the source of strength for a life of robust repentance and rich romance.

THREE BASIC MOVEMENTS

As a pastor I have noticed three basic movements in life. First, there is unorganized selfishness. This describes the bulk of life and history. Blind and bound by sin, people are too backward to learn the art of back scratching: "You scratch my back and I will scratch yours." That is a basic survival skill for a fallen world. But as the philosopher Forrest Gump said, "Stupid is as stupid does." Most of the world, blinded by the god of this world—the devil (2 Corinthians 4:4)—has not graduated from "Gump 101." Only repentance, God's gift created through the message and massage of the cross, and through the means of grace, will lift blinders!

Two, there is organized selfishness. The framers of the United States Constitution defined good government as organized selfishness. "Let's compromise!" "*Quid pro quo!*" "Let's go fifty-fifty!" "Checks and balances!" "Separation of Powers." "Let's work out a plan in the best interest of both parties!" Where people listen to the voice of the Law in their conscience, they can rise to the level of organized selfishness. For a fallen world, that's not bad.

Three, there is this highest form of organization—organized selflessness that Jesus' love brings to us via His Holy Spirit working repentance in our hearts. Via His divine Word and Sacrament, our Lord graciously imparts organized selflessness to marriages. This too is part of the Gospel work of repentance. Because Christ's selfless love begets repentance in human hearts, it moves the heart to selflessness (Philippians 2:3-11; 2:20-21). Where Christ's holy, selfless love descends, one becomes better friends, and this is Good News for millennial marriages (Galatians 2:20; 5:22-24).

[Note: Repentance consists of remorse for our sin (2 Corinthians 7:10); remission of sin by God (Acts 2:38); resolve to do God's will (Matthew 3:8); and rejoicing over the gift of forgiveness of sins (Psalms 51:12). These four "R's" are all part of one movement. They all hang together!]

THE SUPER SUPPER

In addition to the gift of Baptism, God has given the Church another lifeline of love:

It is a meal of forgiveness.
It is the new Passover meal.
It is the Lord's Supper.

Two thousand years ago on Maundy Thursday, the night on which He was betrayed, Jesus instituted a new Passover meal (Matthew 26:17). God's ancient Passover was a rich, redemptive supper. It celebrated the Lord's deliverance of the Children of Israel from Egypt's bonds of slavery. It marked God's angel of death passing over the sins of the firstborn in every household where blood covered the doorposts of their domiciles (Exodus 11).

A MEAL TO HELP US LOVE

The new Passover meal, the Lord's Supper, is a meal that enables couples to live in love and peace through the forgiveness of sins that Jesus Christ brings (Matthew 26:28). It is superior to the old Passover. The old offered the blood of bulls, rams, and lambs. The new offers the very body and blood of Christ. The old pointed to the Gospel. The new is the Gospel. The old brought life-giving Passover blessings to the firstborn of God's Israel. The new brings life-giving Passover blessings to all who are properly instructed and receive it in faith.

Upon proper instruction, Christians partake of the true body and blood of the Selfless One, Jesus Christ (Matthew 26:28). The Early Christian Church in Africa referred to the Lord's Supper simply and sublimely as "life." They realized that this meal, like baptism, offered the treasures from heaven.

THE KEY

At the beginning of this chapter, we quoted Dr. Billy Graham, who said, "The key to a good marriage is two good forgivers." To find the house for this key, one need only look to the household of faith, the Church. Through the Church, Christ has instituted a special office. It is known as the Office of the Keys. Our Small Catechism defines this Office:

The Office of the Keys is that special authority which Christ has given to His Church on earth to forgive the sins of repentant sinners, but to withhold forgiveness from the unrepentant as long as they do not repent.

48

The biblical basis for the Office of the Keys is found throughout scripture, but especially in John 20:22-23. We see here the extraordinary commission authorized by Jesus for the Church "to forgive sins!" The Kingdom of God is a kingdom of forgiveness. In Baptism, the Lord's Supper, and the proclamation of the Gospel, the key to heaven, and to good marriages, is distributed—*forgiveness of sins.* By this, the Church lives and couples love. Lifelines and love-lines together.

Chapter Three

FAITH

.

The hard knuckle-knocking on the door should have warned me that the unexpected visitor was not a happy camper. Without exchanging any social amenities, Mark parked himself in my office chair. Assuming he was counting to ten to gain composure, I waited. The first move would have to come from this man who was not a member of our congregation.

At last he blurted out, "Preacher, I want a divorce!"

Mark's request caught me off guard. His Saturday-morning demand did not add up. A week earlier he was happily chirping when I invited him to an adult instruction class. At that time, no sirens had caught my ear. No smoke signals had caught my eye.

Hoping that Mark's grievance was more a momentary emotional capsizing from a tempest in the teapot rather than a sober flight from a number-five hurricane, I asked him to tell me more.

"What's the problem Mark?" I asked. "Preacher, you won't believe what my wife has done! It's unbelievable! Joan has really gone and done it!" moaned Mark.

From the tone of his voice and the anger on his face, you would have thought that Joan had run off with the butcher or baker—or both! Wanting to get to the core of the complaint, I asked again, "Mark, what's the problem?"

A HAIR-RAISING STORY

Finally, Mark got to the point: "Yesterday, Joan went out and had her long black hair cut. And was it cut short." At this juncture, Mark expected me to break down into wailing and weeping. Instead, I just stared at him. Utterly mystified, I kept looking at Mark, trying to figure out his problem.

As I waited for "the rest of the story," I paused for Mark to flesh out the details of this "grievous ordeal." Maybe his wife had joined the skin heads. Perhaps she converted her hair into a punk-rock Mohawk. Maybe she received a Don King permanent.

No further damaging details came forth. Suddenly, it became obvious that this guy was for real. Mark was about ready to go into a seizure over his wife's shortened hairstyle.

"FOR BETTER OR FOR WORSE" ALTERED

The "for better or for worse" clause in Mark's wedding vows evidently never planned for such a disaster as this. Perhaps his marriage vows should have asked:

"Do you, Mark, promise to live with Joan in the holy estate of matrimony? Wilt thou love her, comfort her, honor her, and keep her in sickness and in health (short haircuts not included) and, forsaking all others, keep thee unto her so long as ye both shall live?"

Mark is not the first husband to go ballistic over his mate getting a short haircut. A friend shared with me the harsh words of a husband to his wife after she received a major clipping from her beautician. Before a gallery of her friends, the thoughtless clod fumed, "I don't know why I had to pay twenty eight dollars to see how ugly you are!"

These hair-raising reactions to the hair-cutting incidents were harebrained to say the least. Added to this, they were *loveless* and *faithless*. Born of hatred and unbelief, they brought nothing but hurt and harm to their mates and marriages.

Faith: "Wedding Ring of the Soul"

It was Martin Luther who said, "Faith is the wedding ring of the soul." Faith in Jesus Christ is also *the* ingredient that keeps wedding rings from leaving married hands. It is a hard saying, but true, that wherever broken promises and broken vows arise, there has been a faith failure. Sometimes, the faith failure is on the part of one spouse. Sometimes, it is on the part of both.

Though this chapter is titled "Faith," it really is at the same time all about love. For like fire and heat, faith and love are inseparable. Where faith in Christ flourishes, love for people pours forth. In fact, faith in Christ makes it possible to love. Wrote C.F. Walther, "For love does not enter a person's heart except through faith." The love of which Walther wrote is *agape* love, the life-giving love of God that flows to us by way of the cross. From the cross this love is delivered through the means of grace, creating faith and *agape* love in human hearts.

Faith and Love — Joined at the Hip!

The Bible makes it clear that faith and love are a wonderful pair of twins. Faith is the driving power. Love is the precious cargo. Listen to the testimony of the Spirit:

> "Since we heard of your *faith* in Christ Jesus, and of the *love* which ye have to all the saints..."
>
> —Colossians 1:4 KJV

> "...*faith* which worketh by *love*."
>
> —Galatians 5:6 KJV

> "Remembering without ceasing your work of *faith* and labour of *love*..."
>
> —1 Thessalonians 1:3 KJV

"That Christ may dwell in your hearts by *faith*; that ye, being rooted and grounded in *love*,..."

—Ephesians 3:17 KJV

Like Spin and Marty, Laurel and Hardy, Tonto and the Lone Ranger, faith and love work together. Someone has said, "Faith is the flower that receives the dew and the sun, while love is the flower reflecting beauty and fragrance." Using a similar metaphor, Richard Lenski adds, "Love is the sacred flower springing from the soil beneath the cross, which was moistened by the Savior's dying blood." Putting it another way, love is the product of faith, and faith is the creation of God's love in Christ.

CONDITIONAL LOVE

By word and deed, Mark gave no evidence that he knew Jesus Christ as Savior. His ludicrous bellyaching about Joan's haircut indicated a bankrupt understanding of the living God and love, for "God is love" (1 John 4:8). His love for Joan was quite unlike God's love for him. God's love toward him was unconditional. Mark's love toward Joan was conditional:

"Joan, I will love you *if* you are pretty."
"Joan, I will love you *if* you are young."
"Joan, I will love you *if* you have long hair."
… An *iffy* love indeed!

AGAPE LOVE

Agape love does not ask, "What's in it for me?" Earlier we noted the great New Testament word for love is *agape*. It is a word rich in meaning and motion. Its source is God. The Apostle John states, "Love is of God" (1 John 4:7).

Christian love, *agape*, depends on love from outside ourselves. This lofty, holy, soaring love does not come to couples naturally, but supernaturally—through faith in the Lord of love, Jesus Christ. Through His Church, He discloses and dispenses this love by repentance, which is the Holy Spirit's work (Acts 2:38-39; Acts 11:18). Consequently, *agape* is love fed by forgiveness.

Agape is the kind of love not motivated by anything loveable in the object of affection. Unlike Mark, who loved Joan because of her long, beautiful black hair, God loved Joan whether she had long hair, short hair, or no hair.

The poet Ovid said, "To be loved, be loveable." That is humanistic hymnody! Contrast it with lyrics of God's love. Says St. Paul, "But God commendeth his love toward us, in that, while we were yet sinners, Christ died for us" (Romans 5:8). *Agape* is love that loves enemies!

It humbles us to see how small our selfish little compasses draw the circle when it comes to love. The perimeters shrink with every condition. Good looks... Money... Nice body... Fame... Right race... Power... Sharp car... Youthfulness... Good athlete... Humorous... Good voice... Intelligent... Long hair... Elite... and more.

HOLLYWOOD LOVE

Have you ever watched those cruel dating shows on television? Numerous contestants, intoxicated by their own egos, verbally knife and carve up potential dates who fail to meet their Barbie-and-Ken-doll criteria. Under the banner of humor, hatred holds its own pathetic little court. Lives are scarred and marred by the ugly, conditional love that labels one person wanted and another person unwanted.

Mother Theresa of Calcutta has said, "Being unwanted is the worst disease any human can ever experience." From God's point of view, there are no little people. God *wants* all people to be saved. Christ died for all people. This is a terrific tonic for people living in a world quick to brand people as undesirable and unwanted.

There is something else about *agape* love. It is holy. *Agape* does not equate lust with love. It is a tough-minded act of the will in conformity to God's will. This latter truth is most helpful in an age when most people don't have a clue as to what love is.

Love: A Definition

Ask most people today what the word "love" means, and they will almost invariably draw a blank. Even after a few minutes of pondering, most will not come up with a useful definition. St. Paul gives us a splendid definition of *agape*: "Love worketh no ill to his neighbor: therefore love is the *fulfilling* of the Law" (Romans 13:10 kjv).

Much of what society today labels as love, the scriptures declare as sin. The Law of God defines adultery, premarital sex, homosexuality, and living together unmarried as disobedience (1 Corinthians 6:9). One of the reasons people wax hazy and fuzzy on the meaning of love is that they don't understand the Law—God's Law. You cannot separate the Love of God from the Law of God. Whatever is lawless is loveless, just as whatever is faithless is loveless (Romans 14:23).

Perfect Love

Scripture teaches that only One Person ever loved perfectly. That Person is Jesus (2 Corinthians 5:21). Adolf Schlatter says, "Here is the one man—the first in history—who not only knew the Word, but did it." Jesus' fulfilling of the Law and loving God and mankind perfectly was just as important as His death on the cross for our sins (Matthew 3:15; 5:17). To Him and His Church we must look in order to seek the source of *agape*.

Agape Love Is Extravagant Love

Furthermore, *agape* love is extravagant. William Sydney Porter, better known as O. Henry, wrote nearly 250 works of fiction. One of his better-known works is a short story called, "The Gift of the Magi." With a surprise ending characteristic of O'Henry's craft, he gives us an insight into the extravagant nature of *agape*.

In the story, a man pawns his favorite pocket watch to buy his helpmate a set of combs for her long, lovely hair. Meanwhile, she has her hair cut to buy him a gold chain for his prized watch. Each gave something precious and priceless for their beloved. In the end, each surprises the other with a demonstration of extravagant sacrifice and extravagant love.

Marriage Is Not a 50-50 Proposition

"The Gift of the Magi" teaches us that when spouses are in love, they give their utmost. They don't scrimp when it comes to love. They don't whittle marriage down to a 50-50 proposition. Their love is extravagant.

Extravagant love will go to endless lengths. Figuratively, people talk about going to hell and back for a loved one. Literally, Jesus did just that for us (Matthew 27:46)! The New Testament says, "This is how we know what love is: Jesus Christ laid down His life for us. And we ought to lay down our lives for our brothers," (1 John 3:16).

"The Extra-mile Marriage"

For a moment substitute the word "spouses" in place of "brothers." Now the verse reads, "This is how we know what love is: Jesus Christ laid down His life for us. And we ought to lay down our lives for our spouses!" Note the sequence, first the lifeline, then the guideline. If husbands and wives pondered and personalized this verse, making it their marriage motto, then what extravagant love would come their way! Such marriages would go the distance because they would have learned from the Crucified One the meaning of going "the extra mile" (Matthew 5:41).

To display extravagant love, people must know they are loved. Psychologist Abraham Maslow says that people who have an inner sense that they are loved are able to, in turn, love. Allow me to cite two examples of men who were recipients of *agape* and dispensers of extravagant love.

HUSBANDS FOR ALL SEASONS: ANDREW AND PAUL

Andrew and Paul were two men who found in Jesus Christ Someone who met their deepest needs: reconciliation with God, cleansing of guilt and sin, the hope of heaven, and the knowledge that they were deeply and unconditionally loved. Because their deepest needs had been met in Jesus Christ, they were men who sought to meet the needs of their respective spouses.

Both Andrew and Paul needed the grace of God (*agape* love) to help them through stretches of their marriage that required a marathon mind-set (Hebrews 12:1). These stretches were thoroughly strewn with thorns and thistles. Hollywood love would not have cut it.

HE DID NOT BAIL OUT!

Andrew's wife, in the prime of her life, came down with an acute nerve disorder. Eventually it confined her to a walker, then a wheelchair, then a bed. Immobile, unable to do the simplest of tasks, for 5,000 days she slowly slid downhill. Every day Andrew stood by her side. I had read that the divorce rate for spouses where one had this disorder shot up to better than 90 percent. Andrew, however, would take the road less traveled. He did not bail out.

Andrew took the hard and high road of love because Someone had walked it before him—Jesus Christ. As the Pioneer and Perfecter of Andrew's faith, Jesus enabled this steadfast husband not to follow his feelings. Instead, walking by faith in the Son of God who loved him and died for him, Andrew found strength and grace through the lifelines of Word and Sacrament.

For over ten years, Andrew accompanied his wife on hundreds of trips to doctors and hospitals. He fed his wife, washed his wife, and tenderly cared for his wife. His was a tough-minded, tenacious, and tender love that was motivated by the love that radiated from the cross. It was this Good Friday love which enabled him to stand by the side of his wife and minister to her even "through the valley of the shadow."

CHRIST'S LOVE CONQUERORS ALL

Paul's commitment to his wife, a woman who died of a lingering and excruciatingly painful cancer, was also a profile of how *agape* love walks the extra mile and makes the extra sacrifice. Paul's love for his wife, a woman who had lost all her hair due to chemotherapy, was sculpted and shaped by the love of His Savior. He was steadfast and immoveable. Whether reading devotions to her, praying with her, feeding her or bathing her, Paul abounded in the work of the Lord" (1 Corinthians 15:58). He was God's mask for this loving task.

On numerous nights, for over 18 months, Paul took in no sleep as he attended around the clock to the needs of his wife. Grounded on the grace of God (*agape*) by lifelines of love (Word and Sacrament) and guided by "Inasmuch as ye have done it unto one of the least of these my brethren, ye have done it unto me" (Matthew 25:40), Paul persevered. Without once murmuring or complaining, he served his wife until the angels took her home to be with Jesus.

Paul's love for his bride of over forty years, and Andrew's love of his bride of twenty-plus years, were marked by an extravagant love created by Christ's love. Fed, they could in turn feed. Through the Church, these spouses found strength for their struggles, food for their souls, and love for their marriages.

THE SUPERNATURAL LOVE THAT GIVES NATURAL LOVE BEAUTY

The importance of *agape* love is that it purifies and fortifies other kinds of love so easily blighted by sin. Too many couples count upon friendship love (*filia*) and sexual love (*eros*) to keep them together. However, due to the infection of sin, the defection of affection can occur swiftly. Sexual love, when mixed with lust rather than *agape*, becomes a breaking force, rather than a bonding force in marriage. Friendship love, when it becomes tested by trials, lacks the sturdiness of God's unconditional love, *agape*.

It is the selfless, giving, holy nature of *agape* that gives human love substance and style. *Agape* properly guides, gears and guards sexual love, while at the same time enriching friendship love. In other words, *agape* strengthens the strands of marriage!

WHERE TO GO FOR LOVE

Where does one go to receive an outpouring of *agape*? In our stressed-out society we need a place to refuel and recharge. The Church is that place. It provides the preaching of the Good News of God's love in Jesus Christ so that you might know that God is for you, and then in turn, that you might be for your spouse.

One of the things I enjoy about being a member of a liturgical church is that our church annually recounts God's saving acts in Jesus Christ. Jesus' birth, life, miracles, teachings, crucifixion, resurrection, ascension, and sending of the Holy Spirit are not just ancient historical facts. Rather, they are acts of God in Christ by which He continues to save not only souls but also marriages.

RESURRECTION REALITIES

The New Testament, by careful use of the Greek verb tenses, emphasizes the *ongoing* power of these ancient acts (e.g., 1 Corinthians 15:4). They are not dead data. They are resurrection realities that account for a tremendous turnaround in lives today.

In Baptism new beings are created (Romans 6:4). In Holy Absolution, the Good News of "no condemnation" (John 20:21-23) frees couples to serve and commend, not exploit and condemn. In the Lord's Supper, intimacy with God leads to intimacy with our spouse (1 Corinthians 10:16). In our liturgy, the carefully-crafted, Scripturally-saturated words of free and full forgiveness direct people to the Lord of love, who in turn enables them to love—Jesus Christ!

Only a nourished spouse can nourish!

Only a spouse who knows he is cherished can cherish!

Only a person who knows she is forgiven can really forgive!

Only a person who knows he is loved can really love!

How often we try to make it through life without continual *agape* outpourings of love!

BIBLE STUDY

While the Lord's day remains the summit point, and the church the summit place for this to take place each week, the Lord wants us to appropriate His grace continually, not sporadically. "Let the word of Christ dwell in you richly!" exhorts St. Paul (Colossians 3:16). "Daily," the early church in Jerusalem watered the plant of faith with the Good News of the Gospel (Acts 2:46).

Because sin, like a beard, grows constantly, we need the grace of God to continually cut it off. Through daily devotions and a

Gospel-centered study of the Word of God, the Holy Spirit provides this divine clipping. Ideally, Christians should try to read the scriptures in such a way that they might each day hear a word of Law and Gospel. These are the two blades by which the Sword of the Spirit slays selfishness and cuts a pattern of selflessness.

"Put On the Full Armor of God"

Martin Luther, ever aware of the dangers of a hit-and-miss study of the scriptures in a life where the devil, the world, and our own sinful desires are ever attacking us, gave this advice. He said, "Therefore, you must be on alert against such attacks and must be fortified on all sides with the Word of God wherever you go or are, in private or in public, in church or at home, at table and in all your associations." The accumulative effect of God's Word through the liturgy, the creeds, the preaching of the Gospel, the sacraments, and daily devotions provides the spiritual arsenal to do battle with the demons of divorce and the dragons of selfishness.

One of our neighbors has a bumper sticker on his car that reads, "God loves you and I am trying too!" An honest admission. Love is hard. Sin is easy. By nature we want ever to ask, "What's in it for me?" *Agape,* the love from above, the love from without, never raises that question!

A Poem Worth Memorizing

In order that the servant part of us maintains the upper hand over the self-serving part, the new nature must be continually fed and the old nature continually bled. A little poem sets forth well this ongoing struggle to appropriate and manifest *agape* love:

Two natures beat within my breast
The one is cursed, the other is blessed
The one I love, the other I hate
The one I feed will dominate.

THE LOVE SUPPER

To help us feed our new nature and therefore truly love, the Lord has given us a love supper. The Church calls this supper "The Lord's Supper." It is a meal, says Augustine, that "demands only hungry souls," souls that hunger to be loved by the God of all grace.

Like Augustine, Luther could not extol enough the benefits of this majestic meal. "By means of this sacrament," writes Luther, "all self-seeking is rooted out and gives place to that which seeks the common good of all." It is a meal that helps the "me" to not get ahead of the "we." For where the "me" gets ahead of the "we," there is always tragedy.

SLAYING EGO MANIA

One of Teddy Roosevelt's children said of the former president, "Father always wants to be the bride at every wedding and the corpse at every funeral." Unfortunately, T.R. wasn't the only person subject to this ego-mania malady. The "me-first" attitude lurks within our hearts, too, and needs to be constantly cast out by the Sacrament of love and repentance (Lord's Supper).

The ruling spirits of marriage today make a cacophony of sounds: "Do your own thing." "If it feels good, do it." "Hold the upper hand." "Stay with them as long as they are beautiful and handsome, healthy and wealthy." We have learned that the unconditional, holy love of God does not make the sounds of "blaring brass or clashing cymbal" (1 Corinthians 13:1 PHILLIPS). Rather, *agape*, a love that proceeds from God, plays a "Hallelujah Chorus." Seen in the person of Jesus Christ and offered to us through His Church, *agape* offers a superior way for couples to walk.

A DESCRIPTION OF LOVE

In the great hymn of love, 1 Corinthians 13, St. Paul describes the way and wonder of *agape*:

This love of which I speak is slow to lose patience—it looks for a way to be constructive.

It is not possessive: it is neither anxious to impress nor does it cherish inflated ideas of its own importance.

Love has good manners and does not pursue selfish advantage. It is not touchy. It does not keep an account of evil or gloat over the wickedness of other people.

On the contrary, it shares the joy of those who live by the truth.

Love knows no limit to its endurance, no end to its trust, no fading of its hope; it can outlast anything. Love never fails.
—1 Corinthians 13:4-8 PHILLIPS

MAYO MEDICINE

At the Mayo clinic there is a statue of four arms. Each arm is of equal length. One arm stands for work; another for worship; another for rest and play. The fourth arm is love. The statue is to remind people of four crucial elements in a person's life if they are to maintain emotional and mental equilibrium. When one arm becomes too long or too short, trouble develops. Tension deficit disorder occurs. We begin to strain gnats or swallow camels (Matthew 23:24). We lose our balance.

It is the fourth arm, love, which, as St. Paul says, "binds everything together in perfect harmony" (Colossians 3:14 RSV). The Church's task is to herald the Good News of God's forgiving love in Jesus Christ, which creates in human hearts the love necessary to love our closest neighbor, our spouse. Luther describes the movement of this love, "A man is placed between God and his neighbor as a medium, which receives from above and gives out again below, and is like a vessel or a tube through which the stream of divine blessings must flow without intermission to other people." This love as it moves along is creative and curing. It creates a closeness where people were once afar. It cures by its healing of divisions.

Dr. Karl Menninger stated, "Love cures people—both the one who gives it and the one who receives it." When the Holy Spirit pours love into our hearts, *agape* love, we can love and be healed on even a deeper level. This love sustains marriages and brings to relationships a measure of how things ought to be. Because this love is a tough-minded, tender act of the will in step with God's will it is intentional. It intentionally seeks to do big little things that build up rather than break down. Edify, not crucify. It ever asks, "What is in the best interest of the whole?" (1 Corinthians 14:3). It is not a sloppy *agape* love, but a love that is smart, prudent, wise, and good-goal oriented. It knows that if you aim at nothing, you usually hit it.

AGAPE'S PATH

By the means of grace, Word and Sacrament, *agape* comes to us through Jesus Christ. Where *agape* abounds, faith flourishes. Where faith flourishes, love thrives. Where love thrives, one finds motivation for carrying out the good "how to" dimensions of love.

An ancient post-Communion prayer captures this connection:

We give thanks to Thee, Almighty God, that Thou hast refreshed us through this salutary gift; and we beseech Thee that of Thy mercy Thou wouldst strengthen us through the same in faith toward Thee and fervent love toward one another; through Jesus Christ, our Lord, who liveth and reigneth with Thee and the Holy Spirit, ever one God, life without end. Amen.

FIDELITY

As a small child, he had committed to memory, "Thou shalt not commit adultery." From the ten Words of Moses he had memorized, "And thou shalt not covet thy neighbor's wife." However, as a middle-aged man, strolling upon a rooftop, these words had drifted to the remote recesses of his mind. The king of Israel was now mulling over other ideas.

The weight of these thoughts did not help King David sleep. He figured an evening walk might ready his head for a pillow. He hoped the night air of the spring might massage a mind feeling guilt. After all, David's troops were risking life and limb in war, and he should have been with them. Instead, he was night-pacing upon the royal rooftop.

LEAVING THE STRAIGHT LIFE BEHIND: TRAGEDY

If David had mixed meditation on the Royal Law (James 2:8) with walking upon the royal rooftop, then he would have been more sure-footed. Instead, the icy path of his idle thoughts sloped his skid into uncontrollable passions. Through the treacherous tricks of the slippery one, the devil, Israel's king veered off the straight road down into the valley of tragedy.

The genesis of David's passions would lead to an exodus of his glory. They would preach a solemn, Solomonic sermon on the gangrene growth of sin when unchecked by repentance. The conception, the gestation, and birth of sin would take David's desires and lead to the death of a marriage, a husband, and a child. This explosion of sin would also lead to years of anarchy within Israel's first family.

WHEN HAVING EVERYTHING IS NOT ENOUGH

St. Louis baseball announcer, Jack Buck, often remarks of prosperous athletes, "They can't stand success." What is true of athletes is true of all people, including princes and kings. The man who slew the giant Goliath, who built a military juggernaut to subdue a string of ancient enemy nations, who had amassed wealth and power, who had seven wives, and who had seventeen children had it all. And yet, having "everything under the sun" was not enough. David's empty soul lusted for more.

As the restless king roamed the rooftop, from a distance his eyes beheld a stunningly-beautiful woman—bathing. A spark of temptation lit David's spiritually-dry mind. David burned with passion.

THE SECOND LOOK ... A LETHAL LEER

A look at an attractive woman is not sinful. But David had gone beyond a look—a second look, a third look. Staring…lusting…leering…wanting to have that which was not his.

Unwilling to be with his troops to wage war, David was now unwilling to wage war with lust. He had not been able to compartmentalize his disobedience to God. In his egotism, he refused to amputate the stare and crucify the lust. He dilly-dallied with sin. No repentance. Without repentance, lust was soon gripping his heart and controlling his head. Unlike Joseph, who fled from the sinful clutches of Potiphar's wife, David danced with lady lust.

The Leaven of Lust

"Blessed are those who are truly sorry for their sin, for they shall see God" is the thought behind the sixth beatitude (Matthew 5:8). Blinded by sin, David did not see God. He continued to stumble into the darkness. Like Raskolnikov in Fyodor Dostoyevsky's *Crime and Punishment*, the leaven of lust gave rise within David to a feeling that he, the king, was above the Law.

Quickly David inquired about this exquisite woman he saw. His servants informed him that her name was Bathsheba, and that she was married to Uriah the Hittite. By now, the sounds of passion had so silenced his conscience that he did not hear she was married. He ordered messengers to bring Uriah's wife to him.

That very night, Bathsheba became the center of David's universe. That very night, he slept with Bathsheba. That very night, lust triumphed over love.

The Highest Mountain

Robert Louis Stevenson once said to an acquaintance: "The most dangerous height which I ever climbed was Mount Ego." David had scaled Mount Ego. His swollen head had caused him to lose his spiritual balance. He dizzily climbed to heights that invited only a fall.

David never regained his former stature after his affair with Uriah's wife. It was not long after his fling that David learned that Bathsheba was with child—his child. With all the energy that his sinful imagination and powerful position could muster, David attempted a cover-up. But trickery and lies did not conceal his deceit. Murder became necessary. Through an unholy alliance with a future blackmailer, David had Bathsheba's husband killed.

THE FALLOUT OF INFIDELITY

In time, David saw his sin. A potent parable by a courageous prophet crushed David's pride. Pardon from God followed. Though the sins of infidelity and murder were forgiven, David's effectiveness as a father, husband, and king took on a noticeable wobble for the rest of his life (2 Samuel 11-12).

There is a French Proverb that says, "Every evil comes to us on wings and goes away limping." David came out of this affair limping badly. The affair robbed him of more than written words can tell.

Indeed, infidelity is a thief. It steals moments and minutes from one's mate and grants them to a third party. It pilfers reputations. It robs people of their integrity. It exchanges a life of honesty for a life of lying and self-justification. It purloins security from one's children.

Adultery spawns another deadly feature. Grave spiritual harm comes about through this act. Adolf Koberle asserts, "Scripture is especially severe in dealing with the sins of the flesh, not only because of their terrible consequences for the companion in sin, but above all they invariably destroy the spiritual gifts of the believer (Galatians 5:19; James 4:4)."

A DIFFICULT ADMISSION, EASY OMISSION

Discussion of matters pertaining to adultery requires high-level diplomacy. Only with precision can one talk about a "guilty" party and an "innocent" party. For example, a few years ago a good friend and I were discussing his first marriage, which was shattered by the infidelity of his spouse. With courage and contrition he mentioned to me, "My sins of omission led to her sin of commission." It was his way of painfully admitting that the affair of his former wife was a signal for help that he failed to see or meet.

Extramarital affairs serve as a barometric reading that volatile pressures have entered or surfaced in the marriage. Sometimes a spouse has very little control over these pressures. Other times a mate's actions or lack of actions help drive the spouse into the arms of another.

TOO LITTLE SEX

Take Cal and Kate. Cal came to my office one day complaining about his wife, Kate. His frustration stemmed from Kate's boycotting him in the bed. With tears Cal said, "If I am lucky, once a month Kate will give me sex. Even then I have to beg her. I am getting tired of begging for what should be a regular part of marriage. I would be happy if we had sex just once a week!"

Kate was furious with Cal when he eventually fell into the charms and arms of another woman. Initially, she could not see how her inactions led to her husband's actions. In time, she saw her contribution to the anatomy of this affair (1 Corinthians 7:3-5).

For what its worth, the eminent cardiologist Dr. Christian Barnard suggests that healthy married couples have as a general target enjoying the act of marriage twice a week. He states that too much sex as well as too little sex can be unhealthy. While in no wise making this the law of the Medes and Persians, his main point is moderation and mutuality. Implied here is thoughtfulness and intentionality to work toward quality time, to keep the courtship going, and to show mutual consideration.

THE MYTH OF THE GREENER GRASS

There are other causes of marital infidelity. J. Allan Peterson, in his fine book *The Myth of The Greener Grass*, says, "Causes of marital infidelity vary as much as the personalities involved, but I believe they can all be considered under one of three general headings: emotional immaturity, unresolved conflicts, or unmet needs."

How many spouses are unfaithful today? Overall, a number of sociologists and sex researchers are predicting that an ever-increasing number of the populace is playing both sides of the bed. Presently, men are less faithful than women. With the rise of more women working outside the home, and the decline of basic values in our society, some experts predict that half of all American women will find the wedding ring of fidelity too heavy to wear.

A SOCIETY SLIDING INTO THE SEWER

It was observed in the previous chapter that Western Civilization has in the twentieth century badly blurred liberty with license, and love with lust. Russian-born Pitirim Sorokin, first professor and chairman of the Sociology Department of Harvard, describes the situation this way: "Our civilization has become so preoccupied with sex that it now oozes from all pores of American life." Small wonder millions of marriages are crashing on the rock of infidelity.

HI-FIDELITY MARRIAGES

Despite this depressing news, there is refreshing news. God's faithful Son, Jesus Christ, grants lifelines of fidelity to help couples maintain hi-fidelity marriages. He who faithfully built the universe out of nothing (Genesis 1:1) faithfully feeds us the hi-fidelity love necessary to withstand the winds of infidelity.

Through the Church, the Spirit of Christ faithfully works to create the love necessary to keep couples committed toward the one-flesh union. When spouses are rooted in the faithfulness of God, the impulses of fidelity grow to combat the Old Adam's eager-to-abandon-promises posture. Through the means of grace God's fidelity becomes our fidelity, His promise-keeping nature becomes our promise-keeping nature, and His faithfulness becomes our faithfulness.

THE COMPONENTS AND OPPONENTS OF FIDELITY

It has been said that getting married is easy, staying married is more difficult, and remaining happily married is the greatest of arts. Understanding the components and opponents of fidelity-fashioned marriages is essential for couples who desire engaging wisely in the art of marriage. To help with that task, an acrostic of the word fidelity will be used to set forth key lifelines and guidelines for marriages high in fidelity. The acrostic reads:

F   Friends
I   Intimacy
D   Determination
E   Elegance
L   Labor
I   Inspiration
T   Temptation
Y   Yes!

FRIENDS

Among other things, writes Dr. William Hulme, a husband and wife should be good friends. Hulme goes on, "The sad truth is that often they are not. Friendship love is perhaps the most difficult phase of married love to sustain."

A poll taken among people who owned dogs gathered tragic-comic results. It indicated that two out of three of these canine couples considered their dog to be their best friend. If the powwow with the bow-wow is taking precedence over friendship within marriage, we have a new twist to the phrase "marriage going to the dogs."

Why Marriages Last

The June 1985 issue of *Psychology Today* carried a refreshing article titled, "Why Marriages Last." The article's authors, Jeannette and Robert Lauer, interviewed 300 couples in marriages lasting at least fifteen years. A number of sound reasons for long-running, lasting marriages were recorded. The couples interviewed affirmed the sacredness of marriage as a union worthy of life-long commitment. They underscored the importance of hard work, setting common goals and having mutual aims. Yet the number one reason for staying together rather than straying apart came from this answer, "My spouse is my friend."

Friendship certainly is a dimension of married love. Lois Wyse, in a short, but lovely poem, comments on this side of love. Her poem "Non-Stop" from *Love Poems For the Very Married* captures a touching aspect about friendship:

Someone once asked me
  To name the time
Our friendship stopped
  And love began

Oh, my darling
  That's the secret
Our friendship
  Never stopped.

Ephesians Four and Five

Two chapters in the Bible that present rich lifelines and excellent guidelines for the building of friendship are Ephesians 4 and 5. I encourage struggling couples to daily read these chapters for three weeks. In addition to containing literature's loftiest section on marriage, Ephesians 5:21-33, these chapters provide formulas for rich friendships.

Actually, the whole book of Ephesians is a gem for marriages and families. Why? It is one of the most sublime compositions of love. Chapters 1-3 tell about God's four-dimensional love (3:18). They reveal how God loved us before we ever were! In love, in Christ, God chose us before the universe was created (1:4). As the Giver of every good gift, God planned our salvation. God the Father authored this plan. Jesus was the agent of this plan. The Holy Spirit administers this plan through the Church (1:3-14). In short, St. Paul reveals the foundation of love (Ephesians 1-3) and then the applications for living from this love (Ephesians 4-6).

A FORMULA FOR CONCORD

One such formula of concord is Ephesians 4:32. Here St. Paul exhorts, "And be ye kind one to another, tender-hearted, forgiving one another, even as God for Christ's sake hath forgiven you." Nothing builds friendships and fosters companionship in marriage like kindness and tenderness. If couples could take the acrimony out of matrimony, there would be a lot less alimony. The best way to take acrimony out of a marriage is to replace it with kindness.

Acrimony tears down. Kindness builds up. The Holy Spirit creates this latter attitude through the Good News of the kindness of God in Christ (Titus 3:4). This kindness seeks to find time for others and searches to meet the needs of others.

Herman Gockel writes, "It is sort of an active kindness that the apostle had in mind; not only a kindness which refrains from doing evil to one's neighbor, but a kindness which is always on the alert, looking for ways to help him and to be of service to him." It is a quality that builds friendship bridges!

SYMPATHY AND EMPATHY

Tenderheartedness also fashions friendship. In marriage the tenderhearted person continually asks, "How can I build up my mate?" Tenderhearted people have time to listen to a problem and reveal sympathy and empathy for another's pain. People say you spell love: T-I-M-E. *Time,* with *tenderness,* is a friendship builder and a fidelity pillar. It is high octane love!

75

Kindness and tenderheartedness. Two potent nutrients to feed fidelity-strong marriages. How do these marriage minerals come to us? They come from the pantry shelf of the fine food of divine forgiveness. Paul's motivation for exhortation of kindness and tenderheartedness is "...even as God for Christ's sake hath forgiven you" (Ephesians 4:32). How well Philip Melanchthon has said it, "We do not love unless our heart is firmly convinced that the remission of sins has been granted to us!"

INTIMACY

Although King David had seven wives, there is no indication that he had a mate with whom he could really communicate. Everyone has a deep need to be understood by at least one person. Had David had one intimate spouse rather than seven casual relationships, the Bathsheba bloodbath would not have occurred. It is precisely because of the lack of one-flesh intimacy that polygamy does not work well.

Steve Inglehart, a colleague of mine, told a group of Christians a story from his missionary experience in New Guinea. Here, polygamy has been the norm for centuries. He said he could tell who the caboose-wife was in the matrimonial train of a certain New Guinean man. She was the one being chased up a hill by one higher in the seniority order. With a long sharp knife, spouse number three hunted bride number four. Now there's an intimacy builder!

Intimately intertwined with intimacy is good communication. Scores of surveys state that the number one reason for divorce is communication problems. Good communication in marriage is uncommon. Paul Tournier writes, "Deep sharing is overwhelming, and very rare. A thousand fears keep us in check. First of all, there is the fear of breaking down, of crying."

Good communication entails a careful chemistry of heaven-born skills. It is saying the right thing in the right manner at the right time in the right dosage. T.S. Eliot noted that people are unable to endure too much reality at once. Indeed, how we need much grace through the means of grace to engage wisely in the art of communication. A wide, Gospel-centered reading of scripture, and a wise, Word-and-Sacrament, congregation-connected life, becomes the means for the Spirit to equip us for every good work.

FEAR DESTROYS INTIMACY

Fear kills communication and destroys intimacy. Within marriage all kinds of fears can easily arise: fear that a spouse will lash out in anger, fear that secrets will not stay secret, and fear that expressed doubts will invite scorn and ridicule. Where this kind of fear is a dominant note, the wrong use of Law will suffocate love.

The way to remove fear is to replace it with faith. Faith helps us to rid the gremlins of the past and ghosts of the future. Fear flees where the love of Christ, through Word and Sacrament, enters. As St. John writes, "His mature love throws out fear" (1 John 4:18). Through Word and Sacrament, fear finds the exit door.

INTIMACY TAKES TIME

In our over-extended and under-befriended age, couples frequently drift apart due to a lack of time together. Intimacy takes time. Just as we need time for the contemplative life that beholds Christ's love, we need time to behold our beloved. The command, "Don't just do something, but stand there," is a needed counterbalance to our fast, frenzied, frenetic life.

Josef Pieper has written a thoughtful book titled *Leisure, the Basis of Culture.* Pieper argues in this little book for the need of leisure-time to think, ponder, and meditate on matters of ultimate truth. When work becomes the center of our universe, a new idol arises chuck-full of enemy surprises. Investing in one's soul, one's marriage, and one's family ought to be the highest priority in life. Intimacy hears the Psalmist's cry, *"Be at leisure—and know that I am God"* (Psalms 46:10).

ONE-DOWNMANSHIP

One of the fears couples express involves fair fighting. Will their mate stick to the issue or go after tissue? Because marriage is the closest of relationships, there is a tendency to try to pull stunts on our spouse that we would never try on anyone else. We must never forget that "a little Hitler" dwells in *every* heart. Humbling, but true (Matthew 15:19). With the Holy Spirit's help we can drown the little Fuhrer—this dictator/salvation by works/control freak side of us. We can drown it through confession of sins and absolution. Remember, this is a lifelong art—continuous, not periodic or episodic. A life of rich repentance is the key, lest our demeanor becomes meaner. When that happens one-upmanship replaces one-downmanship, and marriage begins to slip into some kind of totalitarian control system.

In keeping with my yen to swing into rhyme, I leave you with a little Dr. Seuss on the loose on the subject of fighting a fair fight. To help you fight the good fight (2 Timothy 4:7) of engaging in a fair fight, I hope this little poem sheds some light.

> *The art of a fair fight*
> *Is done best with gentle might.*
> *When bodies are not too tired*
> *And passions not wired.*
> *A good, fair fight stays with the issue.*
> *It does not allow the Old Adam to go for tissue.*
> *Fair fighters know that a soft answer turns away wrath*
> *And often averts a verbal blood bath.*
> *Win-win fighters seek not to boss each other around*
> *Because they realize that's that devil's way to beat down.*
> *Edify not crucify is the way for love to glisten*

That's why fair fighters work hard to really, really listen.
Fair fighters won't dredge up mistakes of the past
Doing that is to fly the flag of forgiveness half-mast!

The guidelines embedded in this homespun poem reflect but a fraction of the wisdom of scripture regarding fighting the fair fight. Wrapped in kindness and tenderness, humility and hugs, forgiveness and forbearance, they provide a context for mutual self-disclosure, hopes, and dreams. These guidelines show us that intimacy does not just happen. Instead, intimacy is part of serious reflection upon God's Law and serious reception of God's Gospel. Clean Law and high-octane Gospel! Regarding the latter, a humble reception of Holy Communion will strengthen the marriage union with power from on high for love here below.

INTIMACY NOT ENMESHMENT

A postscript on intimacy. Don't equate intimacy with an around-the-clock togetherness. Spouses can be too close to each other and, like clinging vines, choke to death one another. A multiplicity of friends contributes to a good, healthy marriage. When I was in New Orleans, there were action/adventure movies that caught my eye, but not my wife's. Neither did she share my zeal for history, nor I her zest for complicated jigsaw puzzles. When it came to the movies, a friend and I would "Siskel and Ebert" them. Meanwhile, she enjoyed the good company of a sister saint. Both of us prospered by allowing the other space in areas of singular interest. Part of intimacy is knowing one's mate well enough not to force her to drink a beverage that is not "her cup of tea."

DETERMINATION

I have always liked what Mrs. Billy Graham said when asked by a reporter if she ever contemplated divorcing her famous evangelist husband. This great woman of faith, with a smile on her face, said, "No, I have never thought of divorcing Billy, but I have thought about murdering him a few times!" It was her witty way of accenting the importance of determination in making a marriage work. Though a partner of a very good marriage, she was keenly aware of the need for tough-minded mutual commitment.

In his work, *The Christian Life*, Dietrich Bonhoeffer expresses a thought that captures the inseparable connection between marriage and commitment. Bonhoeffer said, "It is not your love that sustains the marriage, but from now on, the marriage that sustains your love." Common and deep commitment to one's promises, enriched by God's promises, provides a staying power that sustains love.

In our quick-to-throw-away society, people swiftly dispose of everything from unborn babies to aged adults. It is not surprising that marriage, which falls somewhere in the middle, is also high on the casualty list. The determined effort to make a marriage work today is rarely present when couples tie the knot.

We see this lack of determination in the epidemic problem of couples living together before marriage. Besides being sinful (1 Corinthians 6:9), living together before marriage is an example of a conditional commitment by partners who can't decide if they "love" the other person enough to make an unconditional commitment. No wonder the divorce rate for couples living together before marriage soars to a 50-100 percent higher rate than for those who intertwine sexual intimacy with an *agape* commitment. Yet, with Christ's help via the means of grace (Philippians 4:13), a half-hearted commitment can be replaced by tough-minded commitment.

A Puzzling, Pleasing "I Love You!"

Years ago, a fellow pastor told his wife, "I may not always romantically love you, but I will always be loyal and committed to you!" At first this remark puzzled his mate, but then it pleased her. She understood her hubby's way of expressing how he wanted his love to grow from emotion to devotion.

If a spouse knows one's mate is committed to the marriage, walking on pins and needles and sleeping on egg shells is not necessary; they can breathe easy. Commitment breeds a sense of well-being. A sense of well-being opens the door to communication and intimacy. It is a vivacious cycle riding on trust, not a vicious cycle riding on feelings. Richard Halverson sums up the matter this way. "Relationships are sustained by commitment, not pleasant feelings. Treat a relationship as negotiable, and it's easily lost. Consider it non-negotiable, and a way is found to make it work."

Elegance

Elegance has been described as "refined grace or dignified propriety that expresses good breeding or good taste." It is a quality that couples need to grace all aspects of marriage especially the sexual act within marriage. If this is not done, then the sexual act will likely wedge spouses apart, not weld them together.

G.K. Chesterton once wrote, "All healthy men, ancient and modern, Eastern and Western, know that there is a certain fury in sex we cannot afford to inflame, and a certain mystery and awe must ever surround it if we are to remain sane." Elegant lovers know this. They do not feed on the filth of pornography to lower the marriage act to an animal act. Nor do they force their mate to do that which is painful—physically or emotionally. They have heard the Spirit's call that we are not to "live for ourselves" (2 Corinthians 5:15).

Eros Minus Agape = Sloppy Agape

It is *agape* love that adds elegance to sexual love (*eros*). Without *agape*, *eros* love lacks the rich self-giving dimension that raises the marriage act to a Christ-like act. Marriage run merely on *eros* love, at best, could be termed "organized selfishness."

Tempered with *agape* love, sexual love becomes a beautiful summit meeting of psychological and physical needs. True, marriage helps to restrain this love from the out-of-bounds path so easily taken under the influence of sin (1 Corinthians 7:2). However, under the Gospel, *eros* undergoes a conversion. Under the influence of *agape*, *eros* receives elegance. It becomes for husband and wife a slayer of loneliness, an act that brings life, a means to drive out anxieties, and a way to intimately unite a couple. But elegance must be there!

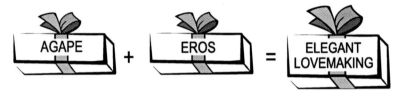

S.O.S. HELP

There is an elegant book in the Bible of 117 verses, written thousands of years ago by a keen observer of humanity. It is a book that meets the S.O.S. needs of romance: *Song of Solomon*. In an elegant manner, Solomon tells the story of two married lovers who court each other with tender touches, lotions and fragrances, sensual words and tantalizing tastes. They realize that wise marriage love is smart, sensitive, and a sanctified seduction that takes work and wisdom.

Elegant love is anything but boring. Song of Solomon couples understand this. Boredom brings burnout. Elegant love is always creative but never kinky. It realizes that variety is not just the spice of life, but an essential part of life itself. For many people, variety comes in a variety of partners; for a Song of Solomon couple, it comes through a variety of creative, elegant actions.

Please note in this book the marvelous mutuality in the right use of the gift of sex within marriage. Please note how each spouse takes turns in initiating the lovemaking. Please note how the picture of Christ's deep love for His Bride—the Church—is unmistakably the beautiful backdrop for the rich reciprocity occurring (Ephesians 5:21-23).

A WHOLESOME APHRODISIAC

In marriage seminars over the years, we have asked the question, "What is it that makes a person sexy to one's mate?" We have heard practical answers: "Keeping up one's appearance." "Practicing good grooming." "Make use of sweet-smelling fragrances." But these are not the chief aphrodisiacs. "Gentleness and kindness are what makes a man sexy," one woman put it. "It is what makes a pretty woman beautiful," said one man. In a word, *elegance.*

Since all good works originate in heaven, we look to God to place into our souls the fidelity bonding agent of elegance. Through Word and Sacrament, "every good endowment" (James 1:17, RSV), including elegance, does proceed. Once again, *agape* plus *eros* equals elegant love-making.

LABOR

Sloth is known as one of the seven deadly sins. Actually, all sin leads to eternal death unless new life in Christ is present (Romans 6:23). In marriage sloth contributes to a deadly drift toward the arms of infidelity. However, love brings to a marriage the initiative, the hard work and sacrifices necessary for a marriage to be a labor of love.

Part of the hard work of marriage involves tough-minded choices. A young man told me the origins of an affair that led to the dissolution of his marriage. It started with a naive agreement to car pool to work alone with a lady. Before long, the twosome's daily trips drew them closer together. From there they crossed the line into adultery. Had the young married man made the hard but appropriate decision to decline car pooling with the woman at the onset, the devil would not have so easily gained a "foothold" (Ephesians 4:27), sending this marriage to the grave.

Pastor David Andrus advises couples that "You enter marriage to serve one another." Translated, "Expect to work hard." He likes to quote Mark 10 where Jesus says, "Anyone who wants to be great among you, let him be your servant" (v. 43). Great marriages are marked by thousands of mutual sacrifices and much hard work and initiative.

Planned Spontaneity

Along this line, Pastor Andrus reminds couples of something he calls "planned spontaneity." To keep the courtship of his marriage going, he will take time and effort to plan surprises and pleasant diversions for his mate. These kinds of things keep a marriage from evolving into a relationship of boredom and "snoredom."

Closely connected with the need for hard work in marriage is the whole matter of discipline. It takes work to discipline one's body and soul. Fidelity demands such discipline. Luther saw the connection when he wrote, "Gormandizing, intemperance, excessive sleeping, loafing and idleness are weapons of unchastity by which purity is speedily overturned." Adolf Koberle adds, "Because chastity is something that affects both soul and body, it requires not only a discipline of thoughts, but also a discipline of the body."

Luther on the Subject of Sex

Discipline plays a key role in the whole realm of sexual relations. Too much sex as well as too little sex can turn this gift into a corrosive rather than cohesive force. The same apostle who said, "Do not deprive one another," in 1 Corinthians 7, said two chapters later, "I discipline my body and make it my slave" (9:27). Speaking to the latter abuse, Luther writes, "It is indeed true that sexual intercourse in marriage should be moderate, to extinguish the burning of the flesh. Just as we should observe moderation in eating and drinking, so pious couples should refrain from indulging their flesh too much." Besides, as one M.D. stated to me, "Less sex is usually better sex." Again, it is all about balance and mutuality and consideration. Recall once more the words of a man who once went way overboard on the matter of sex—Solomon. He wrote as one wiser but sadder, "the man who fears God will avoid all extremes" (Ecclesiastes 7:18 NIV).

Dr. Eugene Peterson in his *The Message* puts this matter into everyday language that one can understand. Drawing from St. Paul's first letter to the saints at Corinth, Dr. Peterson shows how married couples are to be neither ascetic nor self-indulgent. They are to make good, right, and proper use of all the gifts of God for marriage. Quoting St. Paul, Peterson renders with lively metaphor Song of Solomon wisdom to clear up murky reasoning on the matter of sex within marriage:

> *Sexual drives are strong, but marriage is strong enough to contain them and provide for a balanced and fulfilling sexual life in a world of sexual disorder. The marriage bed must be a place of mutuality—the husband seeking to satisfy his wife, and the wife seeking to satisfy her husband. Marriage is not a place to "stand up for your rights." Marriage is a decision to serve the other, whether in bed or out. Abstaining from sex is permissible for a period of time if you both agree to it, and if it's for the purposes of prayer and fasting—but only for short times. Then come back together again. Satan has an ingenious way of tempting us when we least expect it. I'm not, understand, commanding these periods of abstinence—only providing my best counsel if you should choose them.*
>
> —1 Corinthians 7:3-6

INSPIRATION

A New York Times news release had as its headline, "Couples Are Striving Harder to Avoid Divorce." Trish Hall, the author of the article, asserts that divorce is "less attractive these days for reasons like the fear of AIDS and the cost of setting up two households in an uncertain economy." She continues, "Increasingly, marriage is supposed to be worked on, like a car or a roof, often with *expert help*." In recent decades, membership in the American Association for Marriage and Family Therapy has doubled to well over

20,000, indicating that there is more help available for struggling couples. Wherever couples in deep duress can avail themselves of a good marriage counselor as well as a strong Word and Sacrament Gospel-centered ministry, this is well worth the effort. Divorce is so expensive. Granted, sometimes divorce is a tragic necessity. However, blessed is the couple that seeks to get help!

REMEMBER, GOD WORKS THROUGH MEANS

The two words, "expert help," deserve our attention. Inspiration in the form of "expert help" is a good idea. One thing we encourage Christian couples to do is to bring "expert help" into their home in the form of good literature. Ask your pastor to help you purchase a few choice books on the subject of marriage to increase your knowledge. Whether on finances, sexual matters, or communication skills, there are books that will give you insight and inspiration for building a firm family foundation. Attend a marriage retreat as a salutary tune-up to keep the marriage hitting on eight cylinders. Expert help, as noted earlier, can also arrive through a qualified counselor or therapist.

The deepest inspiration and best "expert help" must come from Jesus, through His Holy Spirit, working through the means of grace. Through the sacraments, the Spirit provides the life, love, and lift couples need to serve God and each other. Through the preaching of the Gospel, public and private confession and absolution, and the regular hearing of the good news of God's love in Christ, inspiration is produced. Through these means the Spirit breathes upon us shalom and strength, faith and love, blessedness and beauty (John 20:21-23; 28-29).

This inspiration takes the form of what the scriptures call "the fruit of the Spirit." These lovely gifts from above are: "love, joy, peace, patience, kindness, goodness, faithfulness, gentleness, and self control" (Galatians 5:22). No marriage ever fell apart because of these gifts. However, *it takes two*. One person cannot hold the marriage together. Both husband and wife must be open to being conformed to the image of Christ for marriage to be the beautiful experience that God intends it to be, even in a fallen world context.

The same God Who inspired all scripture (2 Timothy 3:16) inspires Christian couples through that inspired Word. For expert help, wise heads turn to the Creator of the institution of marriage, the triune God. Wise souls seek to follow His guidelines and tap into His lifelines.

AVOID A PICK-AND-CHOOSE METHOD OF BIBLE READING

Some years ago, a pastor asked me a most thoughtful question. "Pastor Kurowski, how is it that congregations can have couples come to church every Sunday, receive the Lord's Supper, hear the Gospel, and attend Bible classes regularly, and yet their marriage is in a shambles?" After a long pause, the Holy Spirit gave me this answer: *"I think you are a Pharisee in the woodpile."*

Many of the Pharisees in the New Testament were known for two destructive practices. One, they loved making the Law-accusing portion of God's Word the dominant note of their theology. In fact, they tortured people with it, suffocated people by it, and placed heavy burdens upon them. In the movie, *The Lion, The Witch And The Wardrobe*, Edmund is a child who does not grow up to be very loving, thoughtful, or kind. Later his siblings learn that it is their strictness, their sternness, their law-accusing behavior that contributes to his lawless behavior. In marriage and family, one needs good clean Law, but the—Gospel in terms of affirmation, confirmation, validation, and freedom—should be the paramount note.

The other destructive practice of many of the Pharisees went hand and fist with their long accusing fingers. When defending their position, it is obvious that they took a pick-and-choose method of Bible interpretation. They strained gnats while swallowing camels (Matthew 23:24). The weightier matters of the law—justice, mercy, compassion and love—they neglected (Matthew 23:23) in favor of their eclectic dialectic.

Lifeline couples realize the danger of a pick-and-choose method of the Bible. They understand that, when it comes to the Bible, if you pick and choose—you lose! They understand that when we pick and choose what we want to believe, we seek to sculpture God into our image rather than vice versa. By nature, the temptation to lawlessly marshal Bible passages with an accusatory edge, to leverage out others in support of a self-serving agenda, is always near.

A full reading of scripture and a Gospel-centered reading of scripture are two measures to counter a warped reading of the Bible. Above all, a continuous contemplation of the thorn-crowned head of the Savior, the cross, and the saving work of Christ will keep the grace of God in the foreground and the Pharisee in the woodpile in the background.

TEMPTATIONS

Temptations to bite the deadly lure of infidelity appear omnipresent. Thomas Boston was not too flattering when he said, "Temptation is the fire that brings up the scum of the heart." To keep the spark of love burning without stoking the fires of filth is an art that only the Spirit of God can teach.

About temptation, Martin Luther quoted the church fathers who said, "Dear brother, you cannot prevent the birds from flying in the air over your head, but you can certainly prevent them from building a nest in your hair." Luther's solution to temptation is direct. "In every temptation simply close your eyes and follow the Word. Outside the Word there is nothing but tribulation."

In recent years Hollywood has spewed out abominable movies that are designed to increase the lure of infidelity and destroy the family. Satan knows that if the family is destroyed, anarchy or totalitarianism is not far away. Hollywood also promotes lifestyles that are death-styles. These death-styles lead to more child abuse—sexual and physical. It remains a fact that a disproportionally high rate of child abuse comes out of the gay community. Does that mean that every gay person is a child molester? No. It does mean, and data will back it up, that the movement as a whole has a much higher percentage of its members who prey upon children. Thus, it is imperative that Christians do everything they can to strengthen marriages and families as a wholesome apologetic to contra-civilization lifestyles.

One Hollywood movie that captured the minds and hearts of many women years ago was titled *Bridges of Madison County*. A woman told me, "I wish every husband was made to see this movie." It was her way of saying how vulnerable spouses can become when the courtship in marriage dies, romance withers, and the Law becomes the dominant note in a marriage.

Granted, *"Bridges"* does teach how sins of omission can grease the slope toward adultery. Also, this movie probably could be a good medium to get the point across to husbands open to that truth. Unfortunately, the movie's main plot sets forth the warped docket of the devil. In *Bridges of Madison County* a wife has a four-day adulterous affair with a photographer while her husband and kids are out of town. The point of this maudlin book written by an economist who knew what sells is sad and pathetic. It suggests how this fling gave the life of this wife monumental meaning and helped her marriage. I suppose that is why they needed a younger Clint Eastwood to play the part of the adulterous photographer. In addition to advancing the sinful "the end justifies the means" philosophy, it whitewashed sin and watered down the deadly consequences of sin.

The Gospel, the remarkable story of God's passionate love for rebel sinners, is the cure, curb, and club for temptations. As citizens of heaven (Philippians 3:20) who live on Temptation Island, we need to be aware of the vultures of temptation that hover around us. The right use of God's Law and a generous portion of the Gospel will help us identify these birds of prey and move a better way.

THE THREE EVIL "A's"

The birds of temptation that wish to nest in our hair are endless. When I speak to confirmation students about the marital pitfalls, I speak of the three evil "A's" that assault marriage: adultery, alcohol, and anger.

Alcohol and anger are not evil in themselves. It is the overuse of the one and the illicit selfish use of the other that makes each destructive. Adultery, of course, is always sin (Galatians 5:19).

Regarding alcohol and drug dependency, the Church must take care to note a temptation inside a cure! In recent years, more and more people have tried to substitute their chemical dependency group for the Church. This is tantamount to substituting it for Christ (1 Corinthians 12:12-27; Hebrews 10:24-25).

Clergy thank God for good chemical dependency centers which help break the grip of drugs on a struggling soul, but we cannot condone substituting that which is good, a chemical dependency center, for that which is better, the Body of Christ! Optimum wholeness can only come about through Christ and His means of grace.

Sinful anger is another destroyer of marriage. It turns specks of sawdust into planks as it maximizes a spouse's sin and minimizes one's own sin. It is hell's humility and it kills communication. In marriage, hotheads produce cold beds. The solution for volcanic selfishness is the realization of one's own staggering load of sin (Matthew 18:21-35), and the awesome absolution that Christ Jesus brings to us (1 John 1:7).

IDEAS HAVE CONSEQUENCES

Another buzzard that tries to nest in our hair is pornographic material. Almost without exception, every man I have interviewed who has fallen into a sexual affair was feeding on pornographic material. Women who also warp their brains with this rot develop pathological thoughts, which can easily become converted into perverted behavior. Likewise, a diet of soap operas with their perpetual "follow your fuzzy feelings" can seduce people's minds before they realize a shift in thinking has even taken place.

For a few years in the 1980's my wife and I watched a half-hour soap opera called *The Bold and the Beautiful*. It started out half-way good. There were decent characters that showed potential for growth. But over time the show got worse and worse. The show kept on dumbing down deviancy. There have been so many incestuous unions in this soap opera that hardly anyone can keep count. Even the ancient pagan Greeks would blush at the kind of immorality that is common on daytime television. Perhaps it is time for *The Bold and the Beautiful* to change its name to *The Porn and the Pernicious*.

Linked to pornographic material is a new lure of infidelity. Dangling from the devil's fishing pole is a new kind of bait. Chat rooms on the Internet have become a net for Satan to use to destroy tens of thousands of marriages. Often the language of the chat room is lurid, salacious, and seductive. Hurting spouses in rocky relationships make a keyboard connection. Innocence gives way to a growing addiction. Prayer and Bible study wanes. Less sleep weakens moral resolve. Reality becomes more of a blur. The twosome thinks they are safe. Distance is on their side. However, they soon engage in an ever more dangerous digital dance. Pain becomes deep common ground. They get to know one another from the inside out—powerful. Pretty soon they throw caution to the wind. They meet. They cheat. The relationship moves from attraction to addiction. It evolves from a faraway keyboard to a nearby bedroom.

Again, remember, God has His means of grace; the devil has his means of disgrace. More often than not, today's chat rooms open the door for the devil to get a ferocious foothold. St. Paul writing to the "saints" at Ephesus (Ephesians 1:1) commanded Christians of all ages to "give no opportunity to the devil" (Ephesians 4:27).

If one cannot always take Philippians 4:8 along on the internet, then one should get off the internet. He who hung on the cross for us, who suffered hell for us, lovingly bids His disciples, "Don't dilly-dally with sin!" To apply our Lord's thinking on this matter we might say, "If the internet causes you to sin, pluck it out and throw it away; it is better for you to lose the internet than that your whole body be caught in the devil's net and be thrown into hell" (Matthew 5:29).

Our first love always influences our second love. Love for the Savior sets the tone for all other loves. John the apostle calls the church at Ephesus to remember their first love—the crucified risen Savior (Revelation 2:4). A deep, daily Christ-centered devotional life, fueled by a Gospel-centered Word and sacrament ministry, and strength from fellowship with members of the household of faith is the dynamic to grow in love as well as avoid a spiritual vacuum. Again, a lot of loving intentionality, robust repentance, and deep dependence upon the *Lifelines of Love* are the keys. Just as our heavenly citizenship makes us better citizens on earth, so does our first Love give contour to the rest of our loves.

Along with internet chat rooms, we should note that the video games today can be a threat not only to marriages, but also to faith formation. Simply the huge amounts of time that occupy a person's attention can make them a god, a center of one's universe. Second, numerous psychological studies are coming out that show these games, especially the violent ones, make people self-absorbed, less sensitive, and prey to being seduced by an ends-justifies-the means ethos. As a pastor I had to visit with a group of young teens that got addicted to video games. They lost sleep. They strayed away from *The Lifelines of Love*. They became isolated. On one occasion, after a long marathon session of a video war game, a disgruntled loser of the game took a knife to the winner. The identity of the young people had become wrapped up in a law move—what one must accomplish to feel good about oneself, versus what God in His Son has accomplished for us by way of the cross.

The Lurid Link

The link between pornography and deviant sexual behavior is more than close. Not only does bad company corrupt good manners (1 Corinthians 15:33), but bad flicks and bad books also corrupt mind and soul. It is so crucial who we have at our elbows, what we view with our eyes, and what we put into our ears. "Avoid sexual looseness like a plague!" (1 Corinthians 6:18 PHILLIPS). That is the apostolic advice. When St. Paul speaks of sexual looseness, it means all its filthy, feathered forms.

We must never forget that the battle begins in the mind before it is lost in the bed. The way to win it is through the daily battle of repentance, crucifying and mortifying the sinful nature through confession and absolution. Rugged repentance will not minimize the sin of flirting or sexual fantasy. It hears the ongoing call of the Spirit, "Examine yourselves...test yourselves" (2 Corinthians 13:5). It sees God's awesome judgment of our sin: "the holy, innocent, bitter suffering and death of His beloved Son, Jesus Christ." Through the gift of absolution, the Christian receives power to walk wisely (Ephesians 5:15) and to seriously pray, "Lead us not into temptation" (Matthew 6:13).

A FAVORITE PRAYER

Over the years I have found the emphasis in the Church's liturgical seasons extremely helpful in encouragement to live a life of repentance. From John the Baptist's Advent call of "sinners to repentance" to the Lenten Hymn, "Jesus I Will Ponder Now," I am continually pointed to the better way. Within one of my favorite prayers to support a life of repentance are the words of this Lenten hymn:

> Grant that I Thy Passion view
> With repentant grieving
> Nor Thee crucify anew
> By unholy living.
> How could I refuse to shun
> Every sinful pleasure
> Since for me God's only Son
> Suffered without measure.
> —Hymn 140, Verse 4, *The Lutheran Hymnal*

There is still another trap that the devil delights in springing. He relishes duping people into immorality by isolating them from the means of grace and Christian fellowship. You see, the tempter can more easily devour Christians when he goes "one on one" with them. However, a strand of three is not easily broken (Ecclesiastes 4:12).

ISOLATION: POOR INSULATION TO TEMPTATION

The devil goes to endless lengths to isolate us from the means of grace, especially from the prime locale of God's face (the church). Is this strategy effective? Very. Philip Zimbardo in *Psychology Today* once wrote, "I know of no more potent killer than isolation...It has been the central agent in the etiology of depression, paranoia, schizophrenia, mass murder and a wide variety of diseased states." This insight, applied to the devil's isolation of a person from the body of Christ, is equally true and eternally more dangerous.

To combat all these temptations, we need to be around the fellowship of God's Word (Acts 2:42). It is through the fellowship of

God's Word, prayer, and Holy Communion that Christian couples become "more than conquerors through Him Who loved us!" (Romans 8:37, NKJV). Through this fellowship we properly "take up the *whole* armor of God" (Ephesians 6:13) to fight off temptation. From Christian fellowship we receive encouragement to draw near to God, and therefore, to our spouse.

FAMISHED MARRIAGES

Today, the deep famine in marriages follows on the heels of a famine of God's Word (Amos 8:11). A lesson that Jesus leaves for us in His victory over the tempter in the wilderness is, "A person will not be kept alive by bread alone but by every word that God speaks" (Matthew 4:4). Apart from continually being fed by the Word, couples will have anorexic strength to love and live. Declares the Church father Jerome, "Therefore, if anyone is not feeding on God's Word the person is not living."

YES!

Each day my wife likes to hear from me, "I love you." It is not a matter of information but affirmation. By nature, because of sin, validation does not roll off our tongues. Through the person of His Son, Jesus Christ, the ultimate affirmation of love takes place. He is God's "yes" to fallen and sinful humanity. He is God's "yes" to our dignity and worth. He is God's "yes" Who moves couples to say "yes" to marriage.

Writes St. Paul: "For God's son Jesus Christ, whom I, Silvanus and Timothy preached to you, was not "yes" and "no," but in Him, "yes" has taken place. For in all the promises of God, He is the "yes" that makes them come true. And so He makes it possible for us to give glory to God by saying, "It is true" (2 Corinthians 1:19-20).

GOD'S YES!

Jesus is this "yes" who creates real friendship (2 Corinthians 5:18-20), regenerates intimacy (Romans 6:3-5), gives us

THE LIFELINES OF LOVE

determination (1 Corinthians 2:2), bestows elegance (Luke 23:34; Acts 7:60), moves us to a labor of love (1 Corinthians 15:58), inspires exciting new life (Galatians 2:20), and who trains us to say "no" to temptation (Titus 2:12).

God's "yes!" of love toward you and me came when His Son died on the cross for our sins and rose again for our justification (Romans 4:25). Intimately the benefits of that "yes" keep on coming to us (Romans 6:3-5) in that "one baptism" (Ephesians 4:5) for the "remission of sins" (Acts 2:38), the Lord's Supper (1 Corinthians 10:16,17), Holy Absolution (John 20:22,23), and through the "message about Christ" (Romans 10:17). This "yes!" teaches us that God is fully for us (Romans 8:31) through His faithful Son, Jesus Christ (Romans 8:32). And God said, "Yes, yes, and yes!"

FREEDOM

The tall man and the short woman were like ducks out of water. Church was not familiar turf to this couple, who looked to be in their upper forties. Sitting in the pew behind them, I had a clear view and close ear to witness their sniping at each other, lack of church etiquette, and crude comments.

Fortunately, the wedding service commenced nearly on time. The two elderly juveniles in front of my wife and me looked like they would be settling down. The music began. The groomsmen and bridal party took their places. The bride came into the church nave on the arm of her father, then the groom escorted her to the altar.

THE MOST MAJESTIC WORDS ON MARRIAGE

After the Trinitarian invocation, the pastor read the most majestic words on marriage in literature: Ephesians 5:21-33. These thirteen verses are the finest combination of lifelines and guidelines of love for a harmonious marriage. Yet something odd happened before my eyes when the sublime words were read. A brawl almost occurred between the short woman and the tall man. Here is what transpired.

The beginning of the Ephesians text reads this way, "Submitting yourselves one to another in the fear of God. Wives, *submit* yourselves unto your own husbands, as to the Lord." At precisely this point in the reading, the foot-taller spouse drove his big bony elbow into the right shoulder of his mate. It was as if he was saying to her, "Did you hear that, Babe?!"

ROLLER DERBY IN THE CHURCH

Her response? She snarled. As she did, she gave him a look that could put a person six feet under. As the reading continued, more roller derby action ensued. The next words, "For the husband is the *head* of the wife, even as Christ is the head of the church: and He is the Savior of the body," drew more movement. Once again the husband cross-checked his wife. She added an extra evil eye to her snarl.

The husband would get in one more lick. As the lector read these words, "Therefore as the church is *subject* unto Christ, so let their wives be to their own husbands in every thing," the husband body banged his mate a third time. Once more, her eyes shot laser beams and bullets of hot anger. Her voice growled.

ROUND TWO

But the action was not over. The turning of the tables was about to take place. The pastor read on, "Husbands, love your wives, even as Christ also loved the church, and *gave* himself for it." With those words, the little woman vigorously poked her husband in *his* rib cage. "Listen up Buddy!" was the clear translation. Now *his* lips wrinkled up with a snarl.

A little later the lector read, "So ought *men to love* their wives as their own bodies. He that loveth his wife loveth himself." Three more rat-a-tat-tat hits to the rib cage were unleashed. Male snarl number two.

The *lex talionis*, the law of retribution, would come after the next verse was read: "For no man ever hated his own flesh; but nourisheth and cherisheth it, even as the Lord the church." For the third time, that feisty little woman let her mate have it in the side. Bang, bang, bang! For the third time, the husband scowled.

BEAUTIFUL BIBLICAL BALANCE

All was "quiet on the western front" until the last verse of the reading: "Nevertheless, let every one of you in particular so love his wife even as himself; and the wife see that she reverence her husband." *Touché. Touché.* No touch. No touch. With long looks they both raised white flags and behaved themselves for the rest of the church service.

THE OMISSION OF DOUBLE SUBMISSION

The omission of *double* submission is one of the biggest problems in marriages today. The call for *both* mates of the marriage to serve one another is rarely heard. Actually, it is an ancient problem as well as a modern day malady. It began when Adam and Eve first refused to submit themselves to God's good orders. Since that day we have had in every generation an ongoing war of the tyrant husband and the rebel wife grabbing for power and control.

It was Dostoyevsky who said, "Men are born rebels." By nature, because of sin, the omission of double submission comes easy to us all. The tall man and the short woman acted out in the pew a struggle that takes place in every marriage. This ancient tug of war was foretold long ago when God said to Eve, "Your desire shall be for that which is of the man, and yet he shall have rule over you" (Genesis 3:16).

By nature, women bristle at this verse as men seek to pound their chest in King Kong fashion. Both are wrong-headed and hard-hearted ways of viewing the relationship that God intends for married couples. Matthew Henry captures the Biblical sense of the husband and wife relationship under God with these lofty words:

> *The woman was made of a rib out of the side of Adam; not made out of his head to rule over him, nor out of his feet to be trampled on by him, but out of his side to be equal to him, under his arm to be protected, and near his heart to be loved.*

One of the saddest comments I have ever heard came from a Christian woman who was married to a man who confused the Biblical order of headship with dictatorship. She said, "My spouse was a better husband before he became a Christian." To understand this otherwise oxymoronic statement, one must understand the spiritually moronic behavior of this husband. It was anything but Christian.

An Exegetical Somersault

When the woman's husband joined the church, he learned that God had placed man as the head over woman in both the home and in the church. This is most certainly true (1 Corinthians 11:3). From there, his power-hungry Old Adam moved him along a devilish path. He then made an exegetical somersault that hurled him into the heresy known as the omission of *double* submission. Without a shred of Biblical support, he concluded that, as the "head" of the house, his word was the final word in all matters of his marriage, regardless of his wife's needs and input. He lapsed into tension deficit disorder. His half-baked conclusion was most certainly false.

"Looking for Loopholes!"

By this leap of lust, the husband graduated from the W.C. Fields school of Biblical interpretation. What I mean is this. In the twilight years of his life, W.C. Fields was spotted thumbing through the Bible. This was odd. Throughout his life, he demonstrated an utter disregard for the things of God. When asked by an onlooker why he was now reading the good book, Fields flippantly whined, "Looking for loopholes!"

There are two major loopholes people invent when it comes to the orders God has designed for the family. First is the denial of any order of headship at all. Second is the omission of double submission.

Those who deny any headship order whatsoever usually will quote a verse like Galatians 3:26-29 which teaches the equality of male and female. But headship and equality are two different concepts. For example, Jesus, though equal to God (John 10:30), places Himself *under* God the Father as His head. Says St. Paul, "But I want you to know that the *head* of every man is Christ, the head of woman is man, and the *head* of Christ is God" (1 Corinthians 11:3, NKJV).

Ultimately there are but three models for husbands and wives to which to submit. There is dictatorship. There is headship. There is the rudderless-ship. The first leads to tyranny while the third ends up in anarchy. *Only* the Gospel-born use of God's gift of headship will keep spouses from making titanic mistakes. Without the gift of headship each spouse becomes a battleship looking to sink the other rather than serve one another. Love is all about meeting the needs of one another. A husband as head uses this gift to be the prime time server in the marriage. A wife who understands this will deeply respect her husband and not take advantage of his servant-hood-headship role (Ephesians 5:21-33). Understood rightly, headship under Christ is a win-win relationship. Understood wrongly, it can deteriorate into double rebellion.

Baptism and Equality

Through this New Testament Red Sea miracle Jesus saves (1 Peter 3:21), sanctifies (Titus 3:5), and sets all Christians on equal footing (Galatians 3:27-28). Indeed, Holy baptism is a mighty, majestic, mysterious, gargantuan Gospel miracle greater than when God created the universe out of nothing (Genesis 1:1)! It has ongoing power that taps into Christ's resurrection and stirs ongoing Easter life into our soul.

Let me be crystal clear on this matter. The scriptures teach the equality of men and women in the sight of God. Nowhere does scripture teach the superiority or inferiority of one sex. While the secular world may teach this, while cultures may advance this, while Christians misusing scripture may promote this, God does not. In Christ, men and women rest on equal footing in the sight of God. Earlier we referred to Galatians 3:26-29. Though it has nothing to say about headship, it does clearly set forth that men and women are equal and the Church is the New Israel. This equal and noble status arises from the Gospel miracle of baptism:

> For you are all sons of God through faith in Christ Jesus. For as many of you as were baptized into Christ have put on Christ. There is neither Jew nor Greek, there is neither slave nor free, there is neither male nor female: for you are all one in Christ Jesus. And if you belong to Christ, then you are Abraham's seed, and heirs according to the promise.
>
> —Galatians 3:26-29

Women, by becoming "sons" of God through faith in Christ Jesus and baptism, stand on equal footing. By declaring women "*sons*," God, through his servant Paul, is using the strongest possible language—language that transcends culture via Old Testament imagery of inheritance—to stress the equal status of men and women. By calling women "*sons*," Paul was declaring a radical, godly, ERA amendment. He was asserting that women and men, in Christ, through baptism, have equal footing in the family of God. This equality in Christ has been called the "order of redemption" by our theologians.

The Often-Forgotten Order

But the order of redemption is not the only order established in Scripture. The Bible teaches that God has set up various orders within the home and the church for the smooth operation of different activities. He has set up these orders to safeguard lives in a world of disorder. These orders are gifts from God. Contrary orders are booby prizes from the devil. As the "God of order," the God and Father of our Lord Jesus Christ wants things accomplished in accordance with His holy will, not our unholy whims.

By nature, we resist the orders of God. When it comes to the order of salvation or redemption, prideful man seeks to obtain salvation by what he does, rather than what Jesus has done. He wants to order salvation by his merits rather than God's mercy.

In matters of life today, "Dr. Death" and the hemlock gang want to order death when it is deemed convenient to them, not pleasing to God. Rather than helping people in their death, they want to help people *to* their death. They want to order the value of people under the umbrella of utilitarianism rather than under the cross and Lordship of Christ (Matthew 25:31-46).

Suicidal Orders

When it comes to the order God has established in sexual matters, man wants to use his freedom to set up new orders. Sex before marriage, sex with children, homosexual behavior, and sex with animals are but a few of the sin-born orders that man has invented. Such orders bring death to the family, death to people, and death to the soul.

In the realm of marriage and the family, power-grabbing, sin-driven spouses want to also pervert God's order—either by the omission of double submission, or ignoring God's order altogether. Unless the Spirit of Jesus dwells within, people by nature are always trying to substitute some human arrangement for God's orders. Done under the guise of liberty, it is usually carried out as license.

It is interesting that in studies done on serial killers, from Jeffrey Dahmer to Ted Bundy, the goal of these mass murderers was power. They did not want to *submit* to anyone. They wanted to create their own order, which led to disorder, and death, pain and tragedy.

A More Excellent Way

Jesus shows us a more excellent way. It is the way of submission. In love, He submits and places Himself under the headship of God the Father. In love, He submits and places Himself under the authority of sinful human beings. Though equal to God and superior to man, He takes the form of a *lowly slave* to free us from the bondage of sin and the slavery of self. So great is His love for the Father and for all mankind that He is willing to submit even to the most painful death in history. The word "submit" is the heart of the Gospel. Paul describes the attitude of Christ to subordinate Himself to save the insubordinate:

> *Do not act out of selfish ambition or with conceit, but in humility think of others as being better than yourselves, while at the same time not being concerned about your own things, but rather about the things of others. Have the same attitude that Christ Jesus had. Although He was God, He did not consider His being equal with God as a prize to be displayed, but He emptied Himself, made Himself a slave, became like other human beings, and when He appeared in the form of a man, He became obedient and humbled Himself even to the point of death, yes, death on a cross.*
> —Philippians 2:3-8 NET

At the heart of the Good News of the Gospel is the *submission* of Christ to the will of the Father. From the virgin womb to the open tomb, He submits to the will of His heavenly Father. What is equally fascinating is what Jesus is going to do on judgment day! After He raises our bodies from the earth, after He reunites them with our spirits, and after He takes us body and soul to the new heaven and earth for all eternity, He is going to submit to the Father for all eternity (1 Corinthians 15:28).

Subject Though Equal

At the end of history, scripture reveals that Jesus will place Himself under the headship of the Father for all eternity! Though *equal* He will be *under* the authority of the Father forever and ever. The model of Jesus in His state of humiliation (Philippians 2:5-11) and for all eternity—to be revealed at the end of history—is the model of submission that husbands and wives are to take. Again St. Paul writes, "Now when all things are made *subject* to Him (the Father), then the Son Himself will also be *subject* to Him who put all things under Him, that God may be all in all!" (1 Corinthians 15:28 NKJV).

The word *subject, (hypotasso)* is one of the monumental words in the New Testament. It is rendered also in English translations as *submit* and *subordinate*. It is a word that describes our Lord. At every point in His life, He submits to His heavenly Father in order to rescue us from the sin and insubordination that has marked and marred history since the fall. When the New Testament uses this word, at no point does it suggest inferiority. At times our English words *subject, submit,* and *subordinate* carry the connotation of inferior/superior. But the Greek word *hypotasso* does not! There is nothing servile or degrading about it. Jesus' actions sanctify it, making it the heart of love.

A Win-Win Situation

In the New Testament, words like *submit* and *headship* are great words. Through the Gospel, they become privileges that flow from faith in Him Who submitted to the cross for us and placed Himself under the headship of the Father. It is the way in which things work best. Certainly these orders as they relate to marriage can become perverted by sin. When a husband refuses to use His headship position to serve his wife, you have the omission of double submission. When a wife uses her freedom to cast away her Christ-like role to submit, she too has perverted God's good order for marriage. When both husband and wife submit to the Gospel call to servanthood, you have a win-win situation. When only one seeks to submit, you have a win-lose situation. When neither submits, you have a lose-lose situation.

One day a colleague and I were marveling over the fact that as you look at the New Testament, Jesus and the Father, though equal, are almost in a contest to see who can give away authority. Christ places Himself under the Father in His state of humiliation. The Father gives Jesus all authority after Easter (Matthew 28:18-20). Jesus places Himself under the Father for all eternity at the end of history (1 Corinthians 15:24-28). Within the Trinity, there is no struggle for power because there is no sin.

A MARVELOUS MARRIAGE MINDSET

"Let this same mindset be in you," writes St. Paul. Where both husband and wife by the Gospel find strength to imitate Christ, oneness will deepen. For where there is "one Lord, one faith, and one baptism," there is mutual oneness to love, which always seeks to serve.

Recall earlier the husband who used his headship to ride roughshod over his wife. He used his headship as a battleship. Consequently he torpedoed his marriage. He took a gift from God and turned it into a tool for a fool. In so doing, he aped the devil, the master at misusing the gifts of God. Moreover, what the husband demanded was not evenhanded. He wanted his mate to be fully subordinate to him without his subordination to God to serve his wife. He wanted to take a circle and turn it into a hubris-built hierarchy. He wanted to use headship as a platform for rights when it really is a foundation for responsibilities. He wanted to be served, but did not want to serve.

A joyful, insightful biography to read is Pastor Ronald W. Stelzer's *Salt, Light, and Signs of the Times*. This inspiring book provides an intimate look at the colorful life and times of one the great heroes of faith in the twentieth century: Dr. Alfred Rehwinkel. Part of Dr. Rehwinkel's greatness grew from his grace-filled marriage to a lady who also was an outstanding heroine of faith—a lady known as Dr. Bessie.

Dr. Bessie's Advice

Dr. Bessie had the right slant on this matter of headship. An M.D., and married to a former Lutheran seminary professor, she used to dispense this advice to young women considering marriage: "Find a man to whom you can easily submit." A man who submits to God is such a man. Submission is always made easier for a wife when a husband submits to Christ's call to sacrifice and serve his neighbor. Who is a closer neighbor than his spouse?

Mutual submission, mutual subordination, mutual subjection—that is the Biblical model. Notice how clearly and closely St. Paul spells out the double submission theme in his letter to Colossians. He leaves no room for a double standard in marriage. "We want to strike a balance" (2 Corinthians 8:13 NET) is the Pauline motto:

"Wives, *submit* to your husbands, as is fitting in the Lord."
"Husbands, *love* your wives and do not be harsh with them."
—Colossians 3:18, 19 NIV

How Do You Spell Love?

How do you spell love? S-U-B-M-I-T! As we learned in chapter three, love is always the submission to God's will (Romans 13:10). Jesus says, "If you love me, you will *submit* to my command" (John 14:15). One of our Lord's commands for Christian husbands is given through the apostle Paul. In the Ephesians text, Paul states that husbands as the head of the house are to love their wives "...just as Christ loved the church and *gave* himself up for her" (Ephesians 5:28).

Einstein's Secret for a Happy Marriage

The proper attitude for leadership by Christian men is embedded in a remark once made by Dr. Albert Einstein. The occasion was the golden wedding anniversary of Dr. and Mrs. Einstein. At that time they were asked the question, "To what do you attribute the success of your marriage?" After a brief pause, Dr. Einstein responded:

> When we first got married, we made a pact. It was this. That in our life together I would make all the big decisions and she would make all the little decisions. And we have kept it for 50 years. That I think, is the reason for the success of our marriage. Then he looked up and added, "The strange thing is that in 50 years there hasn't yet been one big decision."

No marriage will have a good measure of the joy God intended for it unless the spirit of *mutual* acquiescence and *mutual* giving-in flows freely through the relationship. However, if one spouse insists on being a power broker, the chances of the marriage breaking up increase exponentially. It was the church father Chrysostom who said, "The passion for ruling is the mother of heresy." It was the Lord of Lords, Jesus Christ, who said, "Whoever wants to become great among you must be your servant" (Matthew 20:26).

The call of Jesus to servant-hood and subjection runs counter to the path that men and women, husbands and wives normally take. Yet, it is the road to greatness and great marriages. Nothing is more beautiful on earth than the picture of a husband and wife who freely serve one another.

THE PARADOX OF FREEDOM

One of the profound paradoxes in life is that the road to service is the highway to freedom. Marriages that never learn this become enslaved by the chains of self. To serve, a person must be free from the bondage of self, free to live a life of love, free to submit.

In the New Testament, freedom is not some unbridled power to do one's own thing, but the power to serve God and our neighbor. The reason the divorce courts are jammed and marital civil wars are mounting is because people have failed to see the inseparable connection of freedom, subjection, and love. In love, Jesus subjected Himself to the cross to free us from sin and death. In love, Jesus submitted Himself to the curse of the Law to free us to be blessings to each other. In love, Jesus subordinated Himself even unto the bitter pains of hell that we might be freed to sacrificially lay down our lives for our closest neighbor—our spouse!

SERVANTHOOD ILLUSTRATED

LaVyrle Spencer relates a touching story on how servanthood and subjecting ourselves to the needs of others is a marriage builder par excellence. She narrates the story of two brothers remembering the love of their mother and father. The brother speaking is Eric. Here is his precious memory:

> "Remember how it was with Ma and the old man? How at the end of a busy day ... she'd go out there and help him scour down the fish shed?"

> "And the next thing you know they'd be laughing down there. I use to lie in my bed and wonder what they found to laugh about in the fish-cleaning shack at ten-thirty at night. The crickets would be squawking, and the water would be lapping down the boats, and I'd lay there and listen to them laugh and feel so…good…And one time—I remembered this so clearly—I came into the kitchen late at night when all of us kids were supposed to be asleep and you know what he was doing?"

> "What?"

> "He was washing her feet."

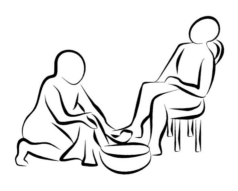

"She was sitting on a kitchen chair and he was on his knees in front of her washing her feet. She had her head back and her eyes were closed and neither one of them said a word. He was just holding her soapy foot above a wash basin and rubbing it real slow with his hands."

Eric paused thoughtfully. "I'll never forget that. Her lumpy old feet that always hurt her so much, and the way the old man was doing that for her."

Once more the two brothers sat in silence, bound by the memory. In time Eric went on quietly. "That's the kind of marriage I want, and I don't have it."

William Penn once said, "Men will obey either God or tyrants." It is the love of Christ that frees us to both know and obey God all the while finding joy in servanthood. As Jesus says, "If the Son sets you free, you are free indeed!" (John 8:36).

LUTHER ON FREEDOM

Martin Luther caught the connection between freedom and subjection. In his tract on Christian liberty, he reminded people of his day that to be free is to submit. He wrote, "A Christian man is the most free, lord of all, and subject to none; a Christian man is the most dutiful servant of all and subject to everyone."

FREEDOM IS FOR THE FREE

The freedom that Luther wrote about was not an external freedom, but an internal freedom; not a political freedom, but a Pauline freedom; not a Jeffersonian freedom, but a Jesus freedom. It was a freedom from something as well as a freedom for something. Luther captured it splendidly in these famous words, "…that I may be His own and live under Him in His kingdom and *serve* Him in everlasting righteousness, innocence, and blessedness."

Freed from the curse of the Law by Jesus, we are free to serve our neighbor. We do this to thank Jesus for His free gift of salvation.

Freed from the fear of death, we are free to live for the one true God and serve our neighbor. Freed from the power of guilt, we are freed for good. And, "What is freedom," asks Hartley Coleridge, "but rightly understood, a universal license to be good?" You see, God's justification of the sinner does not lead to the self-gratification of the saint.

MAMA ZEBEDEE, POWER BROKER

On His final journey to Jerusalem to submit His life to free us from sin, Jesus had an interesting encounter with two of His disciples and their mother. Somewhere along the road to Jerusalem, Mama Zebedee and her two sons, James and John, buttonholed our Lord. Speaking to the spokesperson, Mama Zebedee, Jesus asked, "What do you want?" (Matthew 20:21).

She told Him, "Promise that one of my two sons will sit at Your right and the other at Your left in Your Kingdom." Mama Zebedee wanted her two sons to be top dogs and power brokers in the worldly kingdom she imagined Jesus was about to usher into the history of Israel. Here we have sinful ambition: avarice on stilts.

When the other ten disciples heard about the request of John and James, they were steamed. They did not want to serve these two characters. No second fiddle for them. Just as they started to mix it up with Mama Zebedee's boys, Jesus intervenes.

AMBITION RIGHTLY CHANNELED

Calling his pouting pupils together, He said, "You know the rulers of the Gentiles are lords over them, and their great men are tyrants over them. It is not to be that way among you. Anyone who wants to be great among you, let him be your servant; and anyone who wants to be first among you, let him be your slave" (Matthew 20:25-27).

In paradoxical language, Jesus states that he who would be great in the Kingdom of God shall be so by the power of service. And he who would be first (as did James and John) shall be so by becom-

111

ing a slave of all. The fundamental rule of Christian government is humility and willingness to serve others. This is what makes for good marriages. It is what makes for good friendships. It is what makes for good emotional health.

The cross of Christ produces a spirit that subordinates itself to the will and word of God. Our faith does not free us from submission, but from false opinions about submission. Submission is not subservience or slave morality as the godless philosopher Nietzsche put it. Submission is not the way to salvation for men and women; the submissive Savior alone brings people salvation (Ephesians 2:8-9). In marriage, submission is not a chauvinistic trick to dupe women; rather, *in Christ* it is the path to rich reciprocity and marvelous mutuality.

THE MOST LIBERATING BOOK IN THE WORLD

No book in the history of the world, when rightly proclaimed, has liberated men and women so powerfully and equally as the holy scriptures. When the apostle Peter, for example, declared women to be "coheirs" of eternal life in 1 Peter 3:7, this was about as radical a statement of equality as the ancient world had ever heard. Considering that Aristotle said it was doubtful that women and slaves had souls, Peter's assertion in his day was shocking. "In Rome and Greece," writes Dr. Martin Scharlemann, "women were considered to be chattel." Hence, Peter's proclamation was a colossal countercultural manifesto. Furthermore, Peter's declaration that men who dishonor their wives will not have their prayers answered is a double deterrent to using "headship" for self-serving purposes (1 Peter 3:7).

No book frees men and women to treat one another with mutual respect and kindness like the Bible. Through the lifelines of Word and sacrament, the One who submits to the cross brings Christian couples grace to serve one another. "You were indeed called to be free, fellow Christians," wrote St. Paul, "only do not use your freedom as a launching pad for the flesh; by love continue to serve one another" (Galatians 5:13 NET). Did you catch the connection? Freedom—love—service. They all hang together!

THE SUM OF IT

While the masses either do not know, or sadly abuse, the freedom of faith, true freedom finds expression in loving service to others. The heart is faith in the submissive Savior, Jesus Christ, and the soul is love for God and love for our neighbor. Translated into marriage, freedom shows itself in both husband and wife being about the Father's business of serving one another. I submit to you, therefore, that the finest marriages are composed of two good submitters!

THE PARADOX OF FREEDOM
No gain without pain, sounds insane.
    To submit, I admit, causes me a fit.
A civil war wages as I listen to the sages,
    Who stoke my mind and fire my soul,
And give my heart a different glow.
    To be free…is to wash feet, towel and basin make replete.
Anything less, I confess—tight compress!
    True freedom implies a moral ought, a paradox ever to be
        sought;
Lest liberty suddenly perish… and its license we would cherish.
                                                —Peter M. Kurowski

FINANCES

There is a story about an economist one day bemoaning the fact that he was financially strapped. As a result, he and his wife were at odds. They were having their own battles over the budget. To clear his head, he went for a walk in the woods.

Somewhere along the wooded trail he encountered God. Not knowing what to say, he recalled years before learning that a thousand years was like a minute to the Lord. So he asked the Lord if this was true. And the Lord said, "Indeed, that is true."

Having found God to be a congenial listener, the economist thought he might extend the analogy of time to money matters. "Then perhaps it may also be true that what is a million dollars to us is only a penny to you." The Lord God said, "Yes, that is correct." So the economist said, "Well, Lord, how about giving me one of *those* pennies." The Lord responded, "Certainly, my dear fellow. I don't happen to have it on me, but if you'll wait a minute, I'll go fetch it."

THE FOUR "C'S" FOR A HAPPY MARRIAGE

A pastoral prayer partner of mine, Pastor Nabil Nour, speaks of "the four C's" for a happy marriage. First is Christ. His love is the central theme and golden thread for *Lifelines* couples. Second is the Church. Through the bride of Christ, the Church, the Spirit descends imparting love for a lifetime through the Gospel. Third is commitment. The same Spirit Who led Jesus to the cross provides couples power from on high for here below through the means of grace. The fourth "C" stands for cash. If couples can learn what the Spirit through scripture says about "cash," the marriage journey together will be marked not by the love of money (1 Timothy 6:10), but the love of each other.

Crucial to all of this is to realize that the key to happiness is to forget happiness. When happiness becomes our prime goal it becomes our god. Jesus steers us a far better way. In the Sermon on the Mount He declared, "Seek first the gift of God's Kingdom and the gift of His righteousness and everything else you need will be added to you" (Matthew 6:33, Free Translation). When one's focus is first on the gift of the Kingdom, and the King Himself, heaven's happiness (joy) will follow. However, it occurs as a spin-off of faith rather than as the object of faith. Furthermore, joy is a happiness contingent not upon life's ever changing circumstances, but rather God's infinite unchanging love!

IT TAKES A STEADY HAND TO HOLD A FULL CUP

Often I have told fellow Christians that I wished that they were *all* millionaires—and could handle it. However, it takes a steady hand to hold a full cup, and how easily the love of money can lead to pathological problems. Imagine if more of God's saints had both substantial sums of money to help others, and the gift of generosity! Missions, as well as Good Samaritan projects, provide the salt that preserves our society.

THE WORLD'S VIEW ON MONEY

The world, of course, has a much different view of money matters than the child of God grounded in God's Word. Charles Givens, razor sharp entrepreneur, articulates with gusto the world's view on money. This financial guru asserts, "The real purpose of having more money is to live out your dreams, not just pay your bills."

Behind Given's hard driving, moneymaking methods is a philosophy that is penny wise and pound foolish. It is a philosophy that defines people by what they possess and how many gadgets they gather. It is a creed that confuses the stuff of life with the fluff of life.

Poor Butterfly!

It is not only a western craving to measure the life of people by monetary means, but this malady has captivated Eastern minds as well. Paul Harvey reported a survey taken among Japanese women. They were asked what they seek in a man they wish to marry. The number one answer was money—he must above all be rich. Poor Butterfly!

One of my favorite books in the Bible is Ecclesiastes. Michael Eaton has said this book "...defends the life of faith in a generous God by pointing to the grimness of the alternative." As ancient Near Eastern pessimistic wisdom literature, the book of Ecclesiastes describes the folly of people who make their prime focus in life earthly things. Written by a man who may have been the richest man ever to live, Solomon, the book narrates the sad saga of a king who made money the measure of things. Solomon says:

I amassed silver and gold for myself, and the treasure of kings and provinces. I acquired men and women singers, and a harem as well—the delights of the heart of man. I became greater by far than anyone in Jerusalem before me....I denied myself nothing my eyes desired; I refused my heart no pleasure... everything was meaningless, a chasing after the wind; nothing was gained under the sun.

—Ecclesiastes 2:8, 9, 11 NIV

"What Happened to Their Kids?"

What Solomon experienced is what countless people have learned by chasing the green winds. Malcolm Forbes' book *What Happened To Their Kids* tells of similar replays of Solomon's experiment. Men like William Randolph Hearst, Cornelius Vanderbilt, and John Paul Getty accumulated staggering amounts of money, only to inherit headaches and heartaches.

J. Paul Getty, long considered the richest man in the twentieth century, had five sons from five marriages. Many remember how Getty's grandson, Paul III, on his way home in July 1973 from a discotheque, was kidnapped. A ransom was demanded. When Getty refused to pay a dime, Paul III's right ear arrived in a box at an Italian newspaper office. Money had become the measure of things, and a badly fractured family splintered all the more.

LEARN BEFORE IT'S TOO LATE

A story that received little press in 1991 was the death of former Republican National Committee Chairmen Lee Atwater at the age of 40. Before the age of 40, Atwater accomplished extraordinary political feats and attained extreme power. At his zenith, a brain tumor overtook him. In his weakness, he became strong. Becoming poor in spirit, he became rich in God. Through the Gospel, he came to know Jesus as Savior.

Coming to know Jesus as Savior, Atwater went from "chasing the wind" to be guided by God's Spirit. Atwater found the stuff of life before it was too late. Shortly after his conversion, and not long before his death, Atwater said,

> The '80s were about acquiring—acquiring wealth, power, prestige. I know. I acquired more wealth, power and prestige than most. But you can acquire all you want and still feel empty...It took a deadly illness to put me eye-to-eye with truth, but it is a truth that the country, caught up in ruthless ambitions and moral decay, can learn on my dime.

Don't get me wrong. I am not anti-money when it comes to the family. Having lived in severe poverty, I know first-hand the hardships that come when the cupboards are bare and the pocket purse is empty. Growing up as a child, I recall vividly how my brothers, sisters, and I often stumped nearby town dumps to scrounge food before the rats and rodents ran off with it.

CHRIST-ESTEEM

Though the poorest family in town—people who shopped with vermin—we never felt impoverished. Our personhood was not dependent upon possessions, but the knowledge that the Son of God loved us, died for us, and merited eternal life and forgiveness for us. Not what we had, but Whose we were, was the prime focus we heard from our Gospel-preaching church.

The Bible says "the love of money" is the root of all kinds of evil (1 Timothy 6:10). It is the world's largest slave-holder. Worse yet, the craving for money and mammon can cause people to fall from faith.

"PSHAW"

On the other hand, there is a kernel of truth in George Bernard Shaw's opposite observation that the "Lack of money is the root of all evil." While Shaw's insight may be tainted with a bit of Marxist madness, the scriptures certainly acknowledge evils that can come when financial woes are at one's doorstep. In Proverbs, a treasury chest on money matters, this prayer is given: "Give me neither poverty nor riches, but give me only my daily bread" (Proverbs 30:8). From this prayer I have often prayed, "Lord, don't make me so rich that I become arrogant, and don't make me so poor that I become bitter."

While the prime purpose of the Bible is to make us wise unto salvation through faith in Jesus (2 Timothy 3:15), it also is a book that teaches us practical advice in dozens of other areas. Money is one. To keep us from monetary miseries that lead to marital miseries and family frustrations, God's Word gives all kinds of guidelines on how we should *manage* His money.

WE DON'T OWN SQUAT

And this is precisely what we are—*managers*. We don't own squat. The Psalmist informs us, "The earth is the Lord's, and everything in it, the world, and all who live in it" (Psalms 24:1). Haggai records the Lord as saying, "The silver is mine and the gold is mine" (Haggai 2:8).

A LOOK AT LUKE

Luke, in his Gospel, gives us a story from the lips of our Lord that invites us to be wise managers of what the Lord has given us. Since mishandling money is a major cause of marital failure, the story provides an antidotal attitude to reverse fiscal failure, among other things. The story is known as the Parable of the Shrewd Manager (Luke 16:1-9).

In this story, Jesus tells about a manager who was *accused* of wasting the possessions of his boss. It does not say whether the manager was guilty or not guilty, only accused. The boss tells the manager or steward to turn in his accounts. Realizing that he is about to get a pink slip, he wants to stay in the black and avoid living in the red. Living in a culture where there were no unemployment checks and no social agencies to help, the manager faces a choice. If he fails to plan, he must plan to fail.

Calling in each of the master's debtors, the manager slashes their debt. It is a wise move. By doing this, he is investing in future friends who will be likely to help him down the road. What's vital to note here is that the manager has a right to do this. Basically, he is sacrificing his profit margin to make friends who would help him when he is without work.

SHREWDNESS COMMENDED

Jesus commends the shrewd manager for his prudence and forethought. Our Lord especially praises him for sacrificing money to make friends for the future. Lifting the conclusion of this story to a higher level, Jesus encourages his followers to use God's money to make special friends for eternity (Luke 16:9). Jesus wants us to know that one day in heaven people will welcome us and thank us for wisely using God's resources to bring them the Gospel. The story underscores the truth that, "while many things come and pass, only what's done for Christ Jesus will last!" In other words, use God's money for Gospel bridges and for doing that which will result in positive eternal consequences.

LUKE ON FINANCIAL PRIORITIES

Luke now shifts from prudence to priorities. He wants to instill in us a balanced understanding of the perils, as well as possibilities, of mammon. Thus, in the latter portion of the same chapter, he records the story of the rich man and Lazarus. It is a story that teaches that while wealth is a gift, love of wealth is idolatry. As Luther says in his Large Catechism, "That upon which you set your heart and put your trust is properly your god." The rich man rested his heart on gold, rather than God, and ended up in hell. The whole lesson is a call to teach us to beware of our greed, avarice, and miserliness. It is a call to daily repentance as an integral part of good money management.

LUKE, ONE MORE TIME

A third insight also comes from Luke, M.D. In the twelfth chapter of his Gospel, he narrates a story about seeking the supreme treasures of life. Jesus was talking about life one day. Suddenly, someone stood out from the crowd and boldly directed this request to Jesus: "Teacher, tell my brother to divide the family estate with me" (Luke 12:14).

Scribes or lawyers were often enlisted to mediate and adjudicate such fiscal feuds. Jesus, who came to free people from the craving of covetousness, will not let Himself be drafted in service of man's unholy hankerings. To the man whose supreme treasure was this life, and not the life to come, Jesus said, "Man, who put me over you as a judge or a divider of your goods?" (Luke 12:14).

Then, turning to His disciples, Jesus said, "Be careful and guard against every kind of greed, because even if a person has more than enough, his property does not make his life secure" (Luke 12:15). The man in the text needed not only to make a 180 degree turn with regard to priorities, but concerning his understanding of possessions.

FROM AN M.D. TURNED PREACHER

Dr. Martyn Lloyd Jones, one of England's finest preachers of the twentieth century, put into 37 words a perspective to guide the Christian in money matters. He said, "My whole outlook upon everything that happens to me should be governed by these three things: my realization of who I am, my consciousness of where I am going, and my knowledge of what awaits me when I get there."

Who am I? A person created by God and purchased by the precious blood of Christ. Where am I going? Heaven. What awaits me when I arrive there? Treasures where neither moth nor rust can destroy and where thieves cannot break in and steal (Matthew 6:19).

A GEM FROM C. S. LEWIS

From God's point of view, any discussion on finances must begin with Christ and heaven before our eyes. If not, we will get bogged down with earthly matters. And is there not a marital pitfall here? How often are the fiscal debt problems we have a result of not setting our sights first on God? C.S. Lewis is right when he says, "Aim at heaven and you will get earth `thrown in.' Aim at earth and you will get neither."

Martin Dibelius nicely translated a passage from Philippians that sets our sights properly. Writes St. Paul, "Our home is in heaven, and here on earth we are a colony of heavenly citizens" (Philippians 3:20). In the epistle next door, the apostle enjoins us to "seek the things above, where Christ is seated at the right hand of God" (Colossians 3:1).

LIFELINES AND SALARY GUIDELINES

Both of these words of God remind us that our top priority is to "Seek first the kingdom of God, and His righteousness" (Matthew 6:33). The righteousness of God is beheld in the person of God's Son and comes to us in the Word of God and the sacraments of God. Where these lifelines are the top priority, the salutary guidelines of life have a way of falling into place.

Couples that use their God-given time to be around Word and Sacrament events will have less time and interest for spending money. As one grows in the Word and prospers in sacraments, the materialistic items of this world become less of a priority. As the desire increases to know Jesus better and better, to let heaven fill one's thoughts, and to embrace that which is eternal, the money problems often decrease. Impulse buying gives way to impulses to seek the things of God.

How to Avoid Chasing the Wind

Keeping our priorities straight in financial matters begins with God. It begins with a wholesome preoccupation with the free gift of forgiveness of sins that Jesus brings. It starts with matters of eternal life *first* and *then* temporal life. Failure to make this distinction and one will always be "chasing after the wind."

Saved to Save

As indicated earlier, God's Word is, above all, given to us that we would be saved by grace through faith in Jesus Christ (2 Timothy 3:15). However, God is not just interested in us being saved, but that we might be "equipped for every good work" (2 Timothy 3:17). Properly managing God's money is one such good work!

Often people observe that Jesus spoke more about money than any other subject. Certainly, a good deal of what Jesus had to say was to impress upon us the dangers of making riches the source of self-confidence and pride, the marks of hell.

The Three "S's" of Managing God's Money

In order that we might be shrewd stewards for Christ's cause, God has given us, by way of scripture, much advice on fiscal matters. He has done this that we might create a surplus to fund His work and help His people. Within this advice, there is a huge amount of Christian freedom. With wisdom, prayer, and planning, He wants us to simultaneously *save, share, and spend.*

Unfortunately, most families excel at the latter point and founder in the first two areas.

Take savings as an example. The average man at age 65 years old is up to his eyeballs in debt and owes 22 years on his home to boot. The average American consumer today spends $1.20 for $1.00 earned. Bankruptcies have continued to soar over the years. These are not positions of strength.

CREDIT CARD CRAZINESS

Tragically, most young couples are heading toward even bleaker days. In their attempts to obtain in four years what it took Mom and Dad forty years to buy, they are entering into credit crunch catastrophes. Larry Burkett tells of one individual who had 276 credit cards, stretched out to $1,400,000 of debt.

Mark Twain once wrote a story called "The Terrible Catastrophe." Before he had finished this literary work, he had worked his characters into such a predicament that whatever one of them did, they would be destroyed. At that point, Twain concluded, "I have these characters in such a fix I cannot get them out. Anyone who thinks he can is welcome to try!"

GOOD NEWS FOR MODERN MARRIAGES

This is not a very fair literary device for concluding a story, but it is a familiar financial fix for legions of families. The Good News is that the God who gave His one and only begotten Son to die for our sins is also eager to help us with our financial concerns. Every time we pray, "give us this day" our daily bread, we are asking God to help us order our lives and discipline them in such a manner that we can be good stewards of what He gives us.

To accomplish this, God gives us some general guidelines. The first one is derived from the nature of God. Scripture teaches that God is a God of order (1 Corinthians 14:40). The only way we can manage His money in an orderly fashion is by a budget.

No Course = Off Course

A budget is invaluable in setting up goals, as well as setting limits. Without a budget, expenses can quickly exceed income, bringing about a bad outcome. Some time ago, a person was interviewed on how they managed their household budget. The person said, "I spend 40% of my income on housing, 20 percent on clothing, 40 percent on food, and 20 percent on transportation and amusement." The pollster said, "But sir, that adds up to 120 percent." With chagrin, the man replied, "I know."

Over the years it has been an observation of many pastors that one of the reasons young couples crash on the rock of divorce is the thoughtless, immoral manner in which they pursue financial goals. Undergirding the need for a budget must be this moral truth: "The wicked borrows and does not pay back" (Psalms 37:21). God is not pleased when we steal from others, because of our poor management, lack of discipline, and greed. As people of faith, He wants us to be people of good faith when it comes to paying what we owe.

Budget Beginnings

Now, in developing a budget, where does one begin? Allow me to commend to you three cobblestones as you begin your budget path: prayer, paper, and proper priorities. In the book of James the Spirit of God says, "But if any of you lacks wisdom, let him ask of God, who gives to all generously and without reproach, and it will be given to him" (James 1:4). This first cobblestone, prayer, in the name of the Church's cornerstone, Jesus Christ, is the firm foundation for all budget beginnings. No prayer ... thin air!

The second cobblestone is paper. Simply put, get out some paper and write down your goals. (No course, off course, of course!) On the one hand, list some realistic long term goals. On the other hand, start formulating a budget to cover short term goals (less than one year). Then, on a weekly-to-monthly basis, review the short term goals and on a periodic basis, discuss the long term goals. A *Thrivent Financial for Lutherans* booklet on smart money management says:

> *Short-term goals are important because they force us to restrain from spending money we have right now—something that's not always easy to do. Long-term goals help us establish a plan to save for future purchases—and set aside money to help you work toward long-term financial security.*

The third cobblestone is to set up proper priorities. At the top of the list will be a faith and love commitment to Christ's cause through one's local congregation and other mission outreach programs. However, to get to this commitment, a bit of budget brainstorming must take place.

For a moment let's talk about a few nuts-and-bolts operations necessary in the inaugural stages of the budget brainstorming sessions. An initial step of this process takes place after one has listed one's monthly assets. Next, on paper one should list all the fixed income expenses such as rent, transportation costs, utilities, medical, taxes, insurance, food, clothing, and the like.

Choices must be made as to what can be bought. Christian humility requires mutuality in the decision-making process. It is an invitation to chaos and exploitation for one member of a marriage to make a major monetary decision without conferring with the other spouse. Such an action wars against the one flesh bond of marriage. Frankly, it is an assault on marriage. God will not honor such arrogance, since it violates the golden rule, doing unto others "...as you would have them do unto you" (Matthew 7:12).

Myth: You Can't Have It All

Integral to this budget-making process is a mutual realization that you can't have it all. Millions of baby boomers have had to learn that lesson the hard way. Champagne wishes and caviar dreams should sound fishy when mammon messages are paraded before our eyes and ears. Deferred gratification, one of the great principles of life, is necessary on the part of both husband and wife, lest the credit goblins shackle one with the unbearable weight of debt.

Right From the Top

As part of the budget—right from the top—a generous portion of one's income should go to the work of the Lord. Scripture says, "Honor the Lord with your wealth, with the firstfruits of all your crops" (Proverbs 3:9). In the New Testament, the same principle, of laying aside a generous sum of money in keeping with a person's income is also set forth (1 Corinthians 16:2).

The Open Tomb and Open Pocket Book

The motivation for firstfruits giving is cited by St. Paul in the previous chapter, the great resurrection chapter of the Bible, 1 Corinthians 15. Easter is not only the message of the open tomb, but the motivation for the open pocket purse for the Lord's work. In light of Jesus dying for our sins (15:3) and being raised on the third day, the Christian joyfully gives. We give in light of the fact that one day we, too, will be recipients of a glorified body! Just as Jesus is the firstfruits or foundation of our resurrection, we in turn give Him and His church the firstfruits and foundation of the Father's gifts to us.

An Evangelical Look at the Tithe

Big question. How much shall we give to the Lord from the top? Christian freedom dictates the "how much." Generously, regularly, sacrificially, and proportionately (2 Corinthians 8-9;

1 Corinthians 16:2). These are the New Testament adjectives to describe Christian giving. No fixed percentage is given in the New Testament. While Jesus *commends* the tithe, He does not *command* it (Matthew 23:23).

There are those who insist that 10 percent should be what each Christian couple gives. This may be well-meaning advice but it is wrong-headed advice. This 10 percent figure, or the tithe, as people call it, is based on Old Testament passages such as Malachi 3:10. Here God rightly brings down the law upon a stingy Israel:

> *"But you ask, 'How are we to return?' Will a man rob God? Yet you rob me. But you ask, 'How do we rob you?' In tithes and offerings. You are under a curse—the whole nation of you—because you are robbing me. Bring the whole tithe into the storehouse that there may be food in my house. 'Test me in this,' says the Lord Almighty, 'and see if I will not throw open the floodgates of heaven and pour out so much blessing that you will not have room for it.'"*
>
> —Malachi 3:8-10

Here we must make a careful distinction. We recognize, for example, that for Old Testament Israel the tithe was used to pay expenses that our taxes to the government pay today. Putting it another way, it was somewhat comparable to our income tax. It went to take care of the poor, wage war, and cover a host of expenses (Deuteronomy 14:22, 27-29; Deuteronomy 26:12).

It's nice to think that Uncle Sam would tax us only 10 percent. The carry-over from the Old Testament is free-will offerings, not ten percent offerings. Granted, between you, me, and the fence post, more Christians could afford giving 10 percent to the Church's work. I think the tithe should be a goal for most Christians. However, it is sheer legalism to demand a percent when the New Testament nowhere commands this. Tragically, some Christians are even driven away from the Lord's Supper and attending church by new lawless, lawgiving pastors who ask for something the New Testament does not require.

GOOD GIVERS, GOOD LOVERS

Once a person gives first to the Lord, in light of the cross and in love for the Savior, they are moving in the right direction. Already they are giving to the most important cause of all—getting the Good News of Jesus out and about via the local congregation and other evangelistic enterprises. Notice they are giving. An attitude of giving, born out of love for Him who gave up His life, continues in the home. Where this happens, the giving permeates all relationships. And you know what? Good givers turn into good lovers. And good lovers make for good marriages. Cheapskates simply are not good lovers because they are turned inward rather than outward. Luther stated that is the nature of sin. It is turned inward, self-absorbed, self-centered.

It has been my observation that people who are liberal in supporting Christ's work usually are generous in their love to their children and spouse. Such folks, moved by the mercies of Christ, are sensitive not only to the eternal needs of the lost, but also to the emotional needs of their mate and children. In other words, what one does with their (God's) finances is usually a barometer of their love quotient toward others in scores of other areas. Since the art of marriage is the art of giving, you see how giving first to the Lord sets the tempo and tone for giving throughout the whole marriage. The exception to this is where spouses use sporadic, lavish displays of gifts to control their mate. I have seen this play out in life. However, too much control causes things to spin out of control.

TRUE LOVE CAN'T BE COMPARTMENTALIZED

You can't compartmentalize love. It overflows. Jesus says, "Give, and it will be given to you; good measure, pressed down, shaken together, running over, will be put into your lap. For the measure you give will be the measure you get back" (Luke 6:38).

It was Will Rogers who said, "You can't break a man that don't borrow!" Applied to marriage, it is harder to break up a marriage that does not over borrow. Oh yes, there is constructive debt and destructive debt. Debt on items that will appreciate in value, such as a wisely bought home, a carefully chosen education, or a place for one to implement their vocation, are good investments. Still, the movement, as a rule, should be to pay off all debts.

WESTERN WISDOM FROM AN EASTERN MAN

Nabil Nour, a Lutheran pastor, has taught me much about money management. Born in Palestine, he comes from a culture that imbibes the rich wisdom literature of the Old Testament, so helpful in money management. But it was the words of his South Dakota father-in-law that stuck like glue to my rib cage: "When you borrow, it is as light as a feather; when you repay, it is as heavy as a rock."

Money management experts today encourage people to be careful about the debt they incur when they purchase a vehicle to drive. A brand new car, for example, is probably the worst investment for many people to make. The value plunges 25 to 30 percent the first year. It depreciates 18 percent the second year. The third year, the nose dive continues at 14 percent, 11 percent the fourth year, and 9 percent the fifth year. If one's budget is tight, purchasing a good used car can save one thousands of dollars worth of interest and enable one to have a larger monthly cash flow.

TWO PERSONAL MISTAKES

Two of the biggest mistakes my wife and I have made in finances over the years have had to do with home and automobile. Back in the 1980s, we purchased a brand new car, which we had to junk after the third year because of three transmission problems. In addition to the grief we got from the manufacturers who moved like arthritic turtles in dealing with this lemon, we had nothing but a pile of scrap metal on rubber wheels by the time we paid our 36th payment on it.

What was our mistake? We did not do our homework in buying the car. We failed to read various consumers' reports. We failed

131

to read other automobile books analyzing this model and thus threw down the rat-hole thousands of dollars. We failed to take advantage of the lemon laws that exist to provide a legal corrective. We were poor managers of God's money on this score, due not to greed, but ignorance. Since that time, we have learned to do our homework.

OUR BIGGEST GOOF

Our biggest mistake was buying a house without necessary counsel. Even though we read scads of books on home buying and what to look for, we still paid thousands of dollars more for our first home than what it was worth in respect to the current market value at that time. Even with making a good number of extra principal payments, we still took a heavy financial loss when we sold it. We ended up wiser, but sadder. We have realized the truth of C.S. Lewis' remark that the lazy person must always in the end work a lot harder. We learned a good lesson on prayer and prudence.

PLAN AND PRAY

Our mistakes illustrate a good example of destructive debt. Had we listened to an able ancient entrepreneur, King Solomon, we would not have made this major money mistake. Solomon says, "Plans fail for lack of counsel but with many advisers they succeed" (Proverbs 15:22). Had we done thorough research in purchasing a car, we would have made a better investment. Had we contacted a good real estate person who knew the lay of the land, we would have saved big bucks that could have been used for Christ's cause.

While muffing it badly on our 1982 four-wheel lemon and 1990 overpriced house, by the grace of God we have been more faithful in other management areas. My wife, Janice, does an excellent job at apprising me if we are staying in line with the budget. Once a week, we powwow to make any needed adjustments and sacrifices to put to pasture our debts.

Janice writes out all the bills. Her bookkeeping and budget work have enabled us to be frugal, yet generous. In addition to supporting the local congregation, the Lord has given us a heart to help out single mothers wherever we are able. Like the Proverbs woman (Proverbs 31), Janice looks for sales, uses coupons on sale items, and reads labels carefully so that we can get the same product for less.

For us, credit cards are a tool, not a terror. We pay no interest on anything we buy via the credit card. Year after year, we have made money with a credit card that pays us to use it.

A SCRIPTURAL BASIS FOR SAVING

By God's grace we are moving in the right direction. As we do, our primary goal is to save so that we "...may have something to share with those in need" (Ephesians 4:28). The biggest need is the Gospel. "For what does it profit a person to gain the whole world yet lose his soul?" (Matthew 16:26). Along with the needs of the soul, the Bible tells us that "*as we are able,*" we are to attend to the needs of "all people, but especially to those who belong to the family of believers" (Galatians 6:10). We are to seek to help all people, but with a special emphasis on those of the household of faith. Why? As a rule, members of the household of faith will usually be better managers of Jesus' gifts. Also, when they get on their feet, they tend to be geared more to helping others in turn. In all of this, we do not want to fall into what has been dubbed the tragedy of American compassion, where we give money to people who are reckless in the use of it. Accountability and generosity go hand in hand.

In addition to saving to share, we are also to save for the rainy day. Scripture makes clear that God desires his people to live within the tension of what the Latin fathers called "*ore et labora,*" that is, "work and pray." Work as though it depends upon you. Pray, knowing that ultimately it depends upon God. As Christian farmers have rightly said, "Pray for a good harvest, but continue to hoe." Here is the acknowledgement that workless prayers are worthless prayers.

THE JOSEPH PRINCIPLE

An example of saving for a rainy day (actually for non-rainy days) is a story from the life of the ancient patriarch Joseph. Recall how the Lord made known to him that Egypt was going to be hit with seven bad years after seven bumper harvest years (Genesis 41). As a result, Joseph ordered people to save grain for the lean years to come. Throughout the scriptures, the Joseph principle of saving for the future is commended to us.

By the way, the story of Joseph is one that *Lifeline's* families need to read often, carefully, and prayerfully. It is loaded with deep wisdom (Genesis 37-50). As you recall, Joseph's life was one of peaks and valleys. He went from dreams, to dungeons, to diadems. Adroitly, Moses tells this story with the wisdom God gave him from his years in Egypt. The major point of the story is how God used the gift of forgiveness of sins to break four generations of tragic dysfunction in the family of Terah, Abraham, Isaac, and Jacob. It is a stunning story about family systems, showing the power of divine love, forgiveness, life, and salvation. In the middle of the story is Jesus, the God-Man, helping these patriarchs with blessings of grace (Genesis 18:1-15; 32:22-32). It all hangs together. Don't miss it. It is breathtaking.

Come back to the Joseph principle for a moment. Solomon, in the book of Proverbs, uses the picture of an ant to apply the Joseph principle of saving.

Consider the ant, you lazy bum;
watch its ways and become wise:
Although it has no overseer, officer, or ruler,
in summertime it stores its food supply,
at harvest time it gathers its food.
How long will you lie there, you lazy bum?
When will you get up from your sleep,
just a little slumber, just a little nap.
So your poverty will come upon you, like a drifter,
and your need will come upon you like a bandit.
—Proverbs 6: 6-11, NET

134

The High Cost of Low Living

Throughout the book of Proverbs God grants gems for money management. One theme to ponder is that moral depression precedes economic collapse. The high cost of low living is a killer for families, for communities, and for countries. Briefly, here is a list of moral pitfalls Proverbs teaches as a prelude to a fiscal failure and cultural collapse:

Sloth	Proverbs 10:4; 12:25; 13:4; 14:23
Lack of Discipline	Proverbs 6:23; 13:11
Exploitation	Proverbs 14:3
Lack of Prayer	Proverbs 16:3
Excessive Alcohol/Illicit Drugs	Proverbs 23:21
Adultery/Pornography	Proverbs 6

A Pointer from Pascal

"All the good maxims have been written," wrote Blaise Pascal. "It only remains to put them into practice." A treasury of nuggets on finances and how to manage well what God has given us await the reader of the book of Proverbs. Embedded in this book is the constant exhortation to gain wisdom and knowledge. Wrote Solomon:

"It is not good to have zeal without knowledge, nor to be hasty and miss the way."

—Proverbs 19:2 NIV

"A life frittered away disgusts God; he loves those who run straight for the finish line."

—Proverbs 15:2 THE MESSAGE

"Start with the God of all grace, the God of Abraham, Isaac, and Jacob—that is the first step in learning which also is realizing God is the Giver of every good gift; only fools thumb their noses at such wisdom, grace, and learning."

—Proverbs 1:7, paraphrased

Think and gather information. Think and listen to wise advice. Walk with wise men. Watch your elbows, eyes, and ears. Ponder. Pray. Putting God second is the first big mistake. Begin with the fear of the Lord. Respect deeply His guidelines. Tap richly into His lifelines. All of these messages are words of encouragement to apply to family finances.

HERE'S WALDO!

It was Emerson who said, "The world belongs to the energetic." In saying this he was merely echoing the book of Proverbs, which talks about the need for hard work as the way of wisdom. But hard work must be placed alongside good planning. "For want of skillful strategy an army is lost; the victory is the fruit of long planning" (Proverbs 11:14, NEB). With micro steps, the Christian has macro goals, always aware that goals are to be prayerfully placed in God's hands and based on God's will as revealed in holy scripture. The Bible is our operating manual, interpreter to reality, the cradle of Christ, the love and rescue story, the means by which God speaks to us so that we do not get taken by baloney salesmen, and more!

As one moves toward savings, most counselors encourage couples to develop a savings of at least three to six months' income. Here, diligence is the watchword. Sacrifices are the steps one must take. In working with a number of single mothers, one of the things I have noticed is that they simply lack any kind of game plan to set aside money. When it comes time to buy an appliance they lack money to purchase this item. Often, they have let their heart get the best of them by buying their children things they want, rather than things they need. Thus, when an emergency need arises, they find themselves in want.

Single mothers are not the only ones who struggle with developing a budget, goals, and plans. Research analysts indicate that Baby Boomers in general—the "you can have it all" generation born from 1946 to 1964—are wallowing in fiscal quicksand due to failure to follow a disciplined budget. Analysts reveal that Baby Boomers are heading into a dubious fiscal future:

- 27% don't know what their savings are
- 39% don't know what their company investments really are
- 54% think they will come up short at retirement time
- 3% worry about Social Security being gone by retirement time

MORE WISDOM FROM GOD'S WORD

In the book of Ecclesiastes, God tells his people to save and give for the future. He also tells them, regarding giving and saving, not to put all their eggs in one investment basket. "Give portions to seven, yes to eight, for you do not know what disaster may come upon the land" (Ecclesiastes 11:2). Jim Cramer, a Harvard grad, talk show radio host, and money planning whiz, would ask, "Am I diversified?" In so doing, he is singing what Solomon sang.

As we save, we do not hoard. Neither do we save to accumulate possessions. Keenly aware that the things of this world will all one day be burnt up and destroyed (2 Peter 3:10), we set our sights on a homeland that will last for eternity—heaven (Philippians 3:19-21).

It was written of Faust that he was willing to swap his soul to Satan in return for 24 years of unlimited and unchecked pleasure and power. The Faustian legend has been a saddle a number of composers, poets, and authors have ridden since the Middle Ages. American author Stephen Vincent Benet used this theme in the story "The Devil and Daniel Webster." The Faustian theme reminds us of the age-old struggle not to sell our soul and eternal future for earthly, time-bound pursuits.

A CALL BACK TO LOVE'S LIFELINES

As the Almighty Savior, Jesus graciously bids us to walk with Him, on our way to life in the Eternal City. He helps us with life's thorns, twists, and thistles. He gives us Himself in grace through the prophets, Gospels, and epistles. In particular, He invites us to lay hold of a life-giving, priority-shaping promise. He says, "Seek *first the gift of* His kingdom and *the gift of* His righteousness" (Matthew 6:33) with a promise that all we need will be ours. Here is a call back to the lifelines by which Jesus gives us the treasures of heaven—Word and sacrament. Here is a call to keep the main thing the main thing!

Chapter Seven

FAMILY

M̲ost people realize the strength of a society stands or falls with the family. Through this institution, people yearn to find identity and security. Writing about the family, Robert Frost said, "Home is the place where, when you have to go there, they have to take you in." It is a place God intended as a shelter from many of life's hardships and an oasis for refreshment, where unconditional love would bloom.

Pain

Yet within the family there is—at times—plenty of pain. A television sitcom, "Growing Pains" was an apt title to describe every family. Because all families are composed of the fallen sons and daughters of Adam and Eve, thorns and thistles readily sprout in every home east of Eden.

Growing up in an alcohol-led family of 13, my mother, sisters, and brothers drank deeply the sorrows this cup brings. My father, who was caught in the grips of this liquid demon most of his life, kept the cup of pain quite full as he emptied bottle after bottle. Terrible physical beatings were common. Severe poverty was par.

Sober, my father was a fine man. Drunk, he could become terror incarnate.

THE SINS OF THE FATHERS

His father, too, had been an alcoholic. How true the scriptures are when they talk about the passage of the sins of the fathers going from one generation to the next (Exodus 20:5). Dad would tell us how, when he was a child, his father would order him to run long city blocks to a local store to get a quart of ice-chilled milk to drink in the heat of the night. With sweat running down his face, having run non-stop in order to avoid a beating, my father as a child would watch grandpa drink the whole quart of ice cold milk. Not a drop would be shared with him. For him, family was a place of far more hurt than healing. The law was the dominant note—and bad law at that! Much of that hurt he in turned passed on to us. Karl Menninger was right when he said, "What's done to children, they will do to society." And the bad beat goes on, unless the grace of God intervenes and "new creations" come about (2 Corinthians 5:17).

PARADIGM

Children desperately need good role models. Indianapolis Colts football coach Tony Dungy passionately made that point in light of the suicide death of his son. He reminded football players that, whether they like it or not, they are role models. Actually, we all are. Living in a world where there are so many tormentors (bad law guys) and so few mentors (good gospel guys), Christians must be much more intentional in how we live from the Gospel. We cannot be careless and complacent. The one leads to trouble and the other to tragedy.

A big little thing we can do is to realize the ancient truth of scripture, that truth should be established "in the mouth of two or three witnesses" (Deuteronomy 19:15). With intentionality we need in the mouth of multiple witnesses to say the same thing

(Matthew 28:16-20). Through the Church, the home, and other means-of-grace stations, a three-fold chord is not easily broken. Parents who dump their children off at Sunday school and skip the study of God's Word undercut their efforts for their children to imitate them as they imitate Jesus (1 Corinthians 4:20).

The siblings in my family had a most positive paradigm in my mother. This generous woman could stretch a dollar into a ten spot. She was frugal, yet generous. She also kept father from killing us numerous times when alcohol overtook his faculties. She brought the joy of Jesus into a home that otherwise had major dysfunction and despair written over it.

It was the Church, the bride of Christ, which would provide two more powerful witnesses for me as a child. My best friend Leo had a love for God's Word, the Lord's Supper, and the Savior. His witness helped me immensely. All of this was important for faith formation. Added to Leo's witness was his father's Christ-centered and scripture-centered life. Mr. Bordeleau provided the most positive of role models for me simply by the love and respect he demonstrated to his wife.

How desperately children need a *variety* of good role models. Parents should not let their children simply drift. But as far as possible, parents should make contingencies for God's grace, engage in conversation with them, and show attention. Occasionally, you run into someone who seemingly grows into a strong believer without a multiplicity of good mentors, but this is very rare. It is an exception, not a rule. And the exception should not rule.

A SERMON IN SHOES

Experts say the best thing parents can do for their children is to truly love each other. John's father and mother had no idea that a number of little eyes were watching them mirror Christ's nurturing love toward one another. They were a good sermon in shoes, reflecting the fruits of the Good News.

The Bible presents three types of fathers. Two of these types are poison. The third is a family builder. Leo's father mirrored the third. What are these models? Using Biblical language they are:

- King Saul Fathers   Authoritarian Fathers
- Eli Fathers   Permissive Fathers
- Ephesian Fathers   Nurturing Fathers

AUTHORITARIAN PARENTS

King Saul fathers are authoritarian fathers. They treat their children like a miniature Rodney Dangerfield—with no respect. With Machiavellian method, they rule with iron hand and too many rules. They are critical and carping and controlling.

King Saul, you recall, fit this mold. He did not enjoy being a father. In fact, he even tried to kill his son Jonathan for siding with his beloved friend David. Simply because Jonathan dared to disagree with his father, Saul's anger flared up to the point that he hurled his spear at him to kill him (1 Samuel 20:33). A sick and jealous Saul was addicted to demanding undiscerning obedience from everyone. It is amazing that Jonathan was not more shy, timid, and unresponsive as a result of his authoritarian father. Somehow, the grace of God gave Jonathan a confidence that his always-had-to-be-right father tried to extinguish. Here is comfort that pernicious patterns of the past can be changed. God's grace can mark new beginnings. The impact of the sins of the fathers can be reversed.

PERMISSIVE PARENTS

The opposite of the King Saul father is the Eli paradigm. Eli was a permissive papa. He had trouble setting limits. His two boys, Hophni and Phinehas, grew up to become wicked men who had no regard for right or wrong (1 Samuel 2:12). As a result of being allowed to do their own thing, his boys grew up as wild weeds. They were cruel, self-absorbed predators. Eventually, God's wrath descended upon Eli's two unrepentant sons and they both met death and destruction on the same day.

For decades Dr. Benjamin Spock taught millions of adults to be Eli parents. After reviewing the years of his Phinehas and Hophni heritage, he said "Oops!" and did an about face. In his latter years he advocated the wisdom of discipline, boundaries, and morals as salutary to a child's rearing. He realized that love does not mean you can do your own thing.

THE IDEAL PARENT

The ideal parent, whether male or female, is the Ephesians parent (Ephesians 4:32; 5:21-6:4). This parent is neither too authoritarian nor too wishy-washy. Wise parents seek to avoid being too harsh toward their children (6:4). At the same time, they seek to be nurturing and cherishing (5:29), and kind and compassionate (4:32), training and instructing (6:4) according to Jesus' teachings.

It is an old but true maxim: we learn by what is caught, as well as what is taught. "Children," says James Baldwin, "have never been good at listening to their elders, but they have never failed to imitate them." Today, personified paradigms that reflect and imitate Jesus the Messiah are scarce. "Sermons in shoes" rooted in Jesus' Good News give kids faith-formation clues. They model for our children, and posterity, a life that is in accord with the evangelical Ephesians' example. This little poem drives home this truth:

No written word or spoken plea
Can teach young hearts what to be;
Not all the books on all the shelves,
But what teachers are themselves.

Parents say that peers are their kids' biggest teachers. Kids counter that parents remain the biggest teacher of values. By example, parents remain the prime influence upon their children. Ultimately, Christian parents must tap into power that the Holy Spirit gives through Word and Sacrament!

143

PROBLEMS

The problems of parenting have always been humbling. Howard Hendricks once said, "When finally qualified, I was out of a job!" Looking at the scriptures, you see the struggles of the patriarchal families. Abraham, Isaac, and Jacob all had dysfunctionalism running through their households. David and Solomon faced trial, trouble, and tragedy by the truckload. Adam and Eve had to cope with a murder between their first two children.

In the new millennium the problems that confront parents have heightened considerably. Compare them to the previous generation. For example, teachers 40 years ago were asked, "What were the six worst problems that you faced in working with young people?" Here was their list:

- chewing gum
- making noise
- running in halls
- getting out of place in line
- improper dating
- not putting paper in waste basket

THE DIFFERENCE OF ONE GENERATION

Today the list of problems teachers face, and consequently parents, is drastically different. The six problems listed today are enough to make parents listless. They are:

- drugs
- alcohol
- pregnancy
- suicide
- rape
- assault and battery

Beyond all this there are numerous other social ills. Each day, 1,500 kids drop out of school not having the skills to support themselves in the market place. Each day, 3,300 young people in America run away from home, fleeing into the arms of perverts, drug dealers, and other vultures. Each day, thousands of kids carry a gun to school. Each day, 3,000 teens get pregnant, with over 1,700 choosing not to give the life in the womb a choice.

Indeed, the nuclear family is being "nuked." No wonder many Americans yearn for the past when people understood that freedom and family could only prosper in a nation that had a sense of right and wrong. Is it not interesting that the decade that most Americans believe was the most attractive in our country's history is one that our relativistic cultural elite scorn and sneer at: the 1950s? In his fine book, *Our Journey Home,* Gary Bauer, says of that age:

> The '50s was the decade before radical feminism. Latchkey children didn't exist. The illegitimacy rate was a tiny fraction of today's scandalous 27 percent rate. Abortion was permitted in cases of rape and incest but, for the most part, was illegal in the states. No-fault divorce was still just a gleam in some "reformer's" eye. "Gay" meant happy, homosexuality was "in the closet," and placid "Ike" was in the White House. It was the decade of "Ozzie and Harriet" and "Father Knows Best."

WHY THE DIFFERENCE?

Anyone who has taken the time to study the interplay of Church and life in the history of the United States will note that the 1950's was a time in American history when Christianity deeply impacted our society. As a result, people had a sense of right and wrong through the teaching of the Ten Commandments. In addition, enough of our society embraced the soul-elevating Gospel that the life-giving impulses of this Good News provided the lovely leaven to strengthen our institutions and enhance our culture. While society was as it always is—far, far from a utopia—the family was in far, far better shape than today.

145

PROVERBS

In the chapter on finances, we saw the value of the book of Proverbs. However, its value for the family goes far beyond money matters. It is a rich resource to counter cultural collapse, wallowing in gibberish, and the fall of the family. It is a 3,000 year old guide to family living. In it are some of the best building blocks one can use for laying a firm family foundation.

The first nine chapters of this book are spoken from the viewpoint of a father to a son. The message is to everyone: "Get wisdom at all costs." Since the Hebrew word for wisdom is feminine, you have a book that is inclusive in every sense!

"BAD COMPANY CORRUPTS GOOD MANNERS"

Especially helpful to parents is the divine command from God to young people not to join gangs (Proverbs 1:10-16). Today, gangs have become families for large numbers. These are families that take people to hell. Their creed is: have illicit sex, rip off whomever you can, rape whomever you can, and riot wherever you can. In time, gangs mock God with their disobedience, but in the end God will turn the tables (Proverbs 1:26; 2 Kings 2:24).

The truths of Proverbs are terse comments for all seasons and every culture. It warns against the folly of sex outside of marriage, of lack of discipline, of hot-headedness, of sloth, of lack of repentance, of failure to plan, of pride, and of lack of patience. Here are good attitude builders for parents and quick answers for parents to give to children when they don't have a lot of time to give an elaborate answer.

Most Christians know the name of Zig Ziglar, the motivational speaker and well-traveled Christian author. He once analyzed why our society is faltering and families failing. What he said years ago about Japan applies in many ways to the contrast between education in the East and the West today:

In Japan, starting in kindergarten, for one hour a day until they graduate from high school, students take a course that teaches the importance of honesty, positive mental attitude, motivation, responsibility, free enterprise, thrift, respect for authority, patriotism, and basic values. That's the reason they are eating our lunch in the market place.

GODLY GUIDEPOSTS

A mother was filled with joy one day when she received a letter from her son. In the letter, the woman's son thanked her for teaching him the proverbs of Solomon early in life. It helped him to walk with wise men (Proverbs 13:20). The son, who now has a doctorate in psychology, remarked to his mother how this book continues to help him help others. It is a book that enables him to interpret reality from the light of godly guideposts.

PRAISE

A tremendous builder of families and marriages is the tool of praise. Throughout the scriptures, we see exhortations to praise God, as well as others, for the good works that God works in and through them. Why are parents and spouses so stingy with praise? When one realizes that legitimate praise is one of the most therapeutic things to dish out and receive, why are we so tight, taut, and tentative? Is it because we are letting the Law be the dominant note—and bad law at that?

Note how Jesus vigorously praises Peter for his good confession that Jesus is the Christ (Matthew 16:17). Catch Christ praising the Canaanite woman for her great faith—the faith God bestows (Matthew 11:28). Listen to Jesus commending Mary for choosing that which is best over that which is good (Luke 10:42). Witness St. Paul's praise to God for the congregation that brought him great joy—Philippians (1:3). Mark the words of commendation to the various churches of Asia Minor (Revelation 2-3).

Parents do well to strengthen the family by dispensing plenty of praise as a reward for good behavior. Especially beneficial is praise that connects an act back to the mercies of God in Jesus Christ. The impact of parents praising their children and connecting it to the Good News of Jesus is a staggering transforming tool to the good (Romans 12:1). Here are just a few examples: "John, you are using beautifully the gifts the Savior has given you!" "Mary, the Son of God Who loved you and died for you is greatly pleased by that kind deed!" "Fantastic! The angels in heaven are rejoicing over the thoughtful words you shared with that elderly saint!"

Does that sound stilted? Sure. Is it the normal language we use? No. However, as God's pleasantly peculiar people, we need to be friendly contrarians—not oddballs, but different. We miss so many opportunities to live from the Gospel, to bring Jesus into the conversation, and follow the dandy Deuteronomy doorpost design for faith formation (Deuteronomy 6:6-9). More about that passage later.

Why Don't We Dispense More Praise?

Again, why don't we praise? Partly, we are small on praise because we are big on pride. Daily repentance can help curb and continually cure this. Confessing our sins to God for our paltry praise, we can then praise God for the gift of forgiveness through Jesus. Once we begin praising God for the gift of forgiveness, we are fit and ready to praise our family members for the good things they do by the grace and mercy of God.

The opposite of praise is to label children with cutting remarks. This Jesus exposes as murder (Matthew 5:21-22). Parents who denigrate their children, who tell them they are not smart or pretty, and show favoritism, break the spirit of the child, as well as break the fifth commandment. Jesus has called us to be helpers of joy, not people on a mission to search and destroy.

Child psychologist, R. Urie Bronfenbrenner, was asked in an interview what was the key component in the successful development of a human being. In the twinkling of an eye he said, "Someone, some adult, has to be crazy about the kids." People who are crazy about kids apply the art of praising them as positive reinforcement.

Parameters

The number one problem in schools and homes, experts tell us, is the lack of discipline. Parents spoil their children. They either don't set or don't enforce parameters. With no boundaries or no parameters, children easily go over the edge. The Bible teaches that loving parents will discipline their children (Hebrews 12:6-12), not abuse them.

Love and Discipline

I recall one of God's saints telling me of an incident when she ran into trouble with a policeman for publicly spanking her child one summer evening. House curfew for this child had come and gone. A half hour passed. An hour. Still, Junior was not home.

Junior's mom then went to the nearby park to fetch her son. When she approached him, he began to give her lip. Without opening the topic for debate, she grabbed him by the scruff of the neck, put him over her knee, and proceeded to publicly spank little Mr. Loud Mouth.

About that time, a police car drove up and pulled to a stop parallel to the scene of the spanking. Junior was yapping and yelling as his posterior became better acquainted with mom's palm. The policeman said to Mama Discipline, "Ma'am, don't you think you should ease up on the boy?" Without missing a beat, Mama Discipline told the policeman, "Sir, I am spanking my boy now, so that you don't have to put handcuffs on him later."

Scripture says, "Whoever loves discipline loves knowledge, but he who hates correction is stupid" (Proverbs 12:1). A verse even more familiar is Proverbs 13:24: "He who spares the rod hates his son, but he who loves him is careful to discipline." According to scripture, where there is love there are limits. Though love is limitless in breadth and scope, in matters of right and wrong it spells out limits. With true passion, there are always parameters.

In defining parameters, parents want to avoid two mistakes. First, they want to avoid punishing their children too harshly. Praise should outweigh punishment, and punishment should never morph into child abuse. Second, they want to take time to teach their children. A survey of 3,000 people, taken by *Better Homes and Gardens*, concluded that "an inattentive parent" is the greatest threat to the home.

Perhaps the most quoted portion in the Old Testament is a pa-rameter passage. Deuteronomy 6:4-9, known as the *Shema*, is recited every morning and every evening by orthodox Jews. It teaches that to love the Lord and one's posterity is to set perimeters:

> Hear, O Israel: The Lord our God, the Lord is one.
> Love the Lord your God with all your heart and with
> all your soul and with all your strength.
> These commandments (parameters!) that I give you today
> are to be upon your hearts. *Impress* them on your children.
> *Talk* about them when you sit at home and when you walk
> along the road, when you lie down and when you get up.
> *Tie* them as symbols on your hands and bind them on your
> foreheads. *Write* them on the doorframes of your houses
> and on your gates.

PLAY

Without a doubt, the Bible teaches the importance of hard work. Without hard work and discipline, no person can attain excellence in any art or endeavor. Deferred gratification is a key for pleasure. However, the same scriptures warn about a lifestyle that worships work. From the musings of a miserable man who once was a work-addict we find this verdict, "...but I learned this, too, is a chasing after the wind" (Ecclesiastes 2:3).

What beautiful balance the scriptures present on the issues of life. Work hard, but find time for play. In order that life might not end up in a rut, families need time together to romp and roam, to hike and bike, to picnic and frolic.

FIND TIME TO PLAY

The Mayo Clinic's famous statue of four arms pictures graphically the well balanced life. The four arms are love, work, worship and *play*. When one arm gets too long, the equilibrium of life is lost. We teeter and totter. "I know that there is nothing better for men than to be happy and do good while they live" (Ecclesiastes 3:12). In other words, enjoy life with the grace that God gives you! Find time for play!

Great thinkers of the past have observed the salutary benefits of play. Plato remarked, "You can discover more about a person in an hour of play than in a year of conversation." The father who wrestles with his children on the living room floor, the mother who plays house with her children, and the grandparent who goes fishing with the grandchildren are family builders and future architects of a better society.

G.K. Chesterton, one of the most forceful British writers of the twentieth century, once opined, "The true object of all human life is play. Earth is a task garden; heaven is a playground." It was noted earlier that my father was an alcoholic and at times beat us nigh unto death. Yet when he was sober, he was a good father who knew how to have fun with his kids. From the thousands of fly balls he hit to his nine boys, to the bum's lunches we had together in local parks, to the driving around town in our jalopy station wagon performing our own little Polish hootenanny, we did a lot of playing. How this helped to compensate for those horrific moments of terror brought about by his enslavement to alcohol.

It has been a consistent observation: families that play together tend to stay together. A time to work, and a time to worship. A time to love, and a time to play. Indeed, "there is a time for everything, and a season for every activity under heaven" (Ecclesiastes 3:1).

Prayer

The importance of prayer in the life of a Christian family cannot be underscored enough. Luther said, "What the pulse is to the physical life, prayer is to the spiritual life; to cease to pray means to cease to be a Christian." Like repentance, prayer should be a continuous way of life for the Christian.

Our Lord speaks to us through His Word. We listen. Prayer becomes the speaking back to Him of what He has given to us in His Word. Scripture will always remain the mother of prayer.

Luther reminds us that every time we thoughtfully pray the fourth petition of the Lord's Prayer, we are praying for our family. "Give us this day our daily bread" includes everything and everyone our family needs. Hence, every Lord's Day that we gather to worship in Jesus' name, we pray collectively for our family with the firm conviction that God hears and answers for the sake of His dear Son.

A Lovely Legacy

Teaching children to pray at an early age is a lovely legacy to impart to one's children. At the dinner table, a father and mother can teach their toddler to fold his hands and bow his head, saying simply, "Thank you Jesus for our food. Amen." Simple and sublime.

Parents tell us how they have taught their children the Lord's Prayer already at age two. They tell us how the child will begin participating in the prayers of the church at the youngest of ages.

Prayer changes things. Luther found that God answers prayer. He knew that the greatest tragedy was not unanswered prayer, but unasked prayer. He knew that more was accomplished by prayer than the world dared to dream. In his writings Luther loved to quote James 5:16: "The earnest prayer of a believer in Jesus accomplishes awesome acts."

ZAREPHATH REVISITED
(1 KINGS 17:16)

How often I remember my mother praying to God to help her feed her large family, when there was no "oil in the jar" or food in the cupboards. Though God always answered her prayer, often he made her wait to the last second. Often He answered it in ways much different than we would have prescribed.

One year, come Christmas time, the forecast for our family celebrating in any festive food fashion looked more than bleak. No traditional turkey seemed to be forthcoming. Food supplies were next to nothing. Mom prayed. God delivered. At the last moment, just before Christmas, God sent to the town dump on the eve of Thanksgiving a Red Owl food store truck loaded with frozen turkeys that were "past due" for buyers, but plenty good for us. Wheeling our large two-wheel junk cart to the town, we gathered up all kinds of turkey and trimmings. We brought home that day better than two dozen turkeys and celebrated Thanksgiving for the next two months, able to store the turkeys frozen in our outdoor freezers—the snow banks!

The greatest prayer we can pray is that God will strengthen our faith, for where God strengthens faith, in Christ love grows. Where love grows, the family prospers. With an increase of faith through Word and sacrament, the Holy Spirit gives us coping power for the unexpected problems and unforeseen pains that have a way of entering the back door of every family. Remember, prayer does change things (Luke 11:9-13).

PRESSURES

A friend of mine suggested that I write a few things about stress and the family. The pressures of today, experts tell us, are 40 times greater today than a generation ago. How they compute that I don't know. I do know that the pace of life has quickened. Through a cousin virus of salvation by works, and the fallout of people being treated more like commodities (the fruit of Darwin), folks are stretched into far too many directions. Sleep deprivation is common. Schedules packed to the gills are ubiquitous and iniquitous. Stress from a rise in taxes, from a sharp increase in paper work, and other people not doing their work, adds to the misery index. Thus, through an incremental growth of unhealthy changes, people are extended far more than in the first half of this century. Long discussions with senior saints lead me to this conviction.

Also, the social problems of today are super stress producing. Divorce is stressful. Being a single mother is a Herculean task. Ever-increasing bureaucratic demands don't lighten the load. AIDS, the rise in stealing, homicides, drugs, suicide, terrorism, and sexual predators are all symptoms of a whacked out world where the Gospel is waning and legalism and lawlessness are rising. "I can't take it anymore!" is something we pastors hear all the time and seem to mutter to ourselves more and more. And while CSI television heroes, via the willful suspension of disbelief, can get at the fruits of these matters, only God's guidelines (Law) and lifelines (Gospel) can reach the real roots.

Without trying to play psychologist and psychiatrist, allow me to make some suggestions from God's Word as to how to cope with stress. For starters, talk about your problems to someone. Talk to a good friend or a pastor. As Christians we are to "Bear one another's burdens" (Galatians 6:2), as well as take our concerns to the great burden bearer, Jesus Christ (Matthew 11:28).

CLINT EASTWOOD, THEOLOGIAN

Recognize your limitations. It was Clint Eastwood, as "Dirty Harry," who said in one of his movies, "A man's got to know his limitations." It was Mrs. Dirty Harry who said, "A good woman knows her limits." On a slightly higher plane, the 20th century apologist Elton Trueblood wisely imparted, "Too many commitments amounts to no commitments."

Scripture makes clear that we are clay creatures. We are finite. We have limitations. We need to slow the pace. Psalm 127 teaches us that burning the candle at both ends is not too bright. Get sleep. Streamline your schedule. Remember that there is "a time to keep (commitments) and a time to pitch them" (Ecclesiastes 3:6).

USE SCRIPTURE TO SLAY STRESS

Another suggestion? To slay stress, find choice sections of scripture that are soothing to the soul and give you a heavenly perspective on earthly matters. One saint who daily had a lot of executive decisions to make would read the same three Psalms everyday: Psalm 1, 90, and 103. Each Psalm provided him with a big picture perspective that guided his steps. Here are a few sections of scripture that help prevent countless Christians from losing their equilibrium:

- The 23rd Psalm   The Good Shepherd Psalm.
- The 46th Psalm   A Psalm for time of trouble.
- Habakkuk 3:17-18   A hymn to remind suffering saints that believing is seeing!
- Romans 8   A powerful scripture, assuring us that the best is yet to come!
- Matthew 6   Tremendous therapy for worry! A day at a time: (Little Picture).
- Hebrews 11 & 12   This chapter helps us to keep our eyes on Jesus and not to forget the Eternal City (Big Picture).

Sing Away Stress

Have you ever thought about singing in a choir to alleviate stress? It is a great way to axe anxiety and massage the soul. As a rule, I have noted that people who sing in church choirs tend to be happy campers. Why is this? They constantly store in their head and heart by way of hymns and songs the Good News of God's love in Christ, which always heals and helps the temple! Singing away stress is tremendous therapy. If I were a layman, my "in*choir*-ing" soul would want to go to choir for rest.

Are You Suffering From an Elijah Syndrome?

Proper rest, exercise, and eating well are three other ways to cope with the pressures of life. Do you remember when the great prophet Elijah let the pressures of life overtake him? He got thoroughly disgusted with life. A bout with the blues hit him. Fatigued and filled with fear, he ran for his life from wicked Queen Jezebel and her puppet husband, Ahab (1 Kings 19).

What is fascinating is the *sequence* of steps God takes to restore Elijah. First, God deals with Elijah's fatigue. It was Vince Lombardi, the famous Green Bay Packer football coach, who said, "Fatigue makes cowards of us all." To help Elijah with his fear and fatigue God allows him to crash into a deep sleep (1 Kings 19:5). Then God sends an Angel to wake the prophet up giving him a nice high energy, low fat, and low cholesterol meal (1 Kings 19:6).

Next, God puts Elijah to sleep again. He slowly recharges his batteries. Once more he feeds him. Following this, he puts Elijah on a good exercise program, sending him on a forty-day hike to Mt. Horeb (1 Kings 19:8). After rest, good food, and an exercise program, God comes to Elijah in the gentle voice of His Word to give him the big picture. For good measure, God puts the previously isolated prophet back into fellowship with other believers. Now Elijah is ready to roll up his sleeves again.

What I have set forth in simple commentary from this fascinating story of pressure points in the life of one of God's prophets is what any good stress management expert would tell you. And it's all in God's Word. Eating well, resting well, exercising well, and fellowshiping with the saints are all ways to take care of the temple of the Holy Spirit.

SUPERNATURAL STRESS REDUCERS

The prime procedure for coping with pressures is this: the Holy Spirit strengthening us through Word and Sacrament. This is the soul food we need, along with the good body food we obtain from a wise diet. The Church, through its Bible study programs, its Gospel-centered liturgies, and its offering of the Good News through the sacraments, prepares for God's people a diet to help us cope and give us hope. For stress reduction, we stress a Gospel preaching church. Here the life-lines of love and healing, Word and Sacrament, provide the spirit with the grace it needs for the problems it faces.

FINAL FOOTNOTES ON STRESS

The actress Mary Lou Henner once said, "the key to life is how well you handle Plan B." I think the key is how well you handle plans C, D, and E. A deep conviction of God working all things together for our good (Romans 8:28), i.e., Good Friday tragedy leads to Easter Sunday triumph, is God's pattern for the Church (Ephesians 1:20-23). If God took the worst day in human history since the fall—Good Friday—and worked it together for the good, then He will certainly help us with plans B, C, D, and E! The wounds of Christ and the sword of the open tomb assure us of this Good News.

Also, one of the things every Christian must learn is how to give up the good for the better and the better for the best. Remember, the devil will do all he can to wear us out physically and spiritually. Gospel-centered Sabbath rest for the soul and sufficient Sabbath day rest for the body are two fundamental needs for everyone. Intentionality is the watchword. Along with this, the Church must guard against exaggerated activity as well as lethargy. We remember continually how the devil tempts us with opposites.

Pardon

In chapter two, forgiveness is revealed as the key to a good marriage. Similarly, it is the great glue to a strong family. Other glues are also important. But with forgiveness comes knowledge of Christ's love, which in turn enables family members to love. With forgiveness comes the apron of humility, which is the prettiest clothing family members can wear (1 Peter 5:5). With forgiveness comes repentance, and the Holy Spirit, who is always building up what sin is trying to tear down (Acts 2:38). With forgiveness comes a reversal of decay and deterioration (Luke 7:4). There *is* power in pardon.

Motherly Wisdom

Not long ago, a mother spoke to me about how she has noticed her children apologizing to one another more frequently. Confession of sin, and pardon, are a regular part of the conversation in this family. The kids have heard their parents say, "I am sorry" to each other almost daily. They have heard their parents apologize to them. In the awareness of Christ's forgiveness, they also heartily forgive each other, burying old sins, commencing new beginnings, and manifesting the inseparable love toward each other that comes with forgiveness of sins. Through the mutual pardoning of each other, ongoing healing keeps this family healthy and whole.

Pardon is necessary for another reason. Every conscientious parent will tell you the deep guilt they feel at times for not being able to provide their children with the very best. They realize that they fail to sufficiently say, "I love you." Hugs and words of affirmation don't come as easily and frequently as they should. Time does not allow them to listen and be available nearly as much as they would like. On other occasions, they wish they could provide them with things that their children's friends have. They regret the harsh words and cross looks.

Thank God, the renewing gift of forgiveness of sins keeps us from drowning in guilt. On Sunday after Sunday we hear this Good News from the pulpit. We take, eat, and drink it in the Lord's Supper. We are reminded of it in the liturgy, and we receive it from the public absolution of sins by the pastor in Christ's stead. Sabbath after Sabbath, we hear the Good News from Christ's called ambassador: "Jesus Christ came into the world to save sinners!" (1 Timothy 1:15). This is news that every member of the family needs to hear continuously, so that we might be freed to live the abundant life.

PATTERNS

One of my favorite movies/musicals is "Fiddler on the Roof." In that production, a Russian peasant named Tevye goes into a thoughtful discourse on the importance of traditions—or, here I shall say, patterns. To not have traditions, Tevye asserts, is to walk through life on unsure footing, to be no better than a "fiddler on the roof!" Tevye's point is this: where traditions quickly are lost, families quickly disintegrate.

While our major identity in life comes from whose we are (and not what we do), what we do flows from whose we are. Because we are children of the heavenly Father, adopted in baptism, and members of the New Israel through faith in Jesus (Galatians 3:26-29), we live from this Good News in certain patterns. From the sturdy tradition of Christ rising from the dead on the third day, we live life with joy and hope. Because this is the source of optimism in our world view, certain practices, traditions, and patterns develop accordingly.

Allow me to illustrate this. In our household, we like reading Psalm 90 the minute the New Year begins. We do this to remind ourselves that, while we do not know what the future holds, we do know who holds the future—our eternal and merciful God. Like many other Christian households, we enjoy reading the Christmas story in the King James Version before opening the presents. We pray when we sit down to eat. We call and write loved ones on a regular basis. These traditions or patterns define who we are, give order and fixed points to our life, and create memories.

For other families different traditions might define who they are and what their priorities are in life. Reading Bible and bedtime stories is a precious pattern in many households that gives children lovely memories of the past and rich hopes for the future. Having meals and meaningful discussion at the dinner table might be a time and tradition that brings strength to another family. To preserve family values, to remember one's heritage, and to remember who we are and why we are here, these patterns of life are props of enormous significance.

"Plugged Into"

The critical importance of "plugging" into a life living from the lifelines of love came to me in February of 2001. I was asked to be one of the three judges for selecting the Missouri Mother of the Year. The American Mother of the Year Society is an excellent group of women who uphold the critical importance of domestic engineers. Get to know them and support them wherever you can!

The two top contestants in the Missouri 2001 finals were both superb mothers, as well as sagacious grandmothers. What was striking about them was a similar trend. Each loved her children and grandchildren with deep, unconditional love. Each had gone through many a severe trial as she was sculpted through adversity into a beautiful woman. Third, each of these mothers was closely connected to the lifelines of love offered in her local congregation.

As I marveled at God's wonderful work in their lives, I thought also of Luther's insight as to what made a person a good theologian and a mature Christian. Luther stated that trial, meditation upon Christ's love and the Scriptures, and prayer were the tools the Holy Spirit used to conform us into the image of Christ. Once again, we see the close connection between lifelines and loveliness.

Perhaps some of you saw the adventure film, *Indiana Jones and the Last Crusade*. In this action-packed thriller, Jones begins a dual search for his father and the Holy Grail. As you may know from the study of medieval history, the Holy Grail is a tale about the purported cup Jesus used at the last Supper. There is no Scriptural basis for this story line, so my interest is curious rather than serious. However, what I will say is that, in baptism, the Lord's Supper, holy absolution, and the preaching and teaching of the Gospel, we have treasures infinitely more majestic, more powerful, and more awesome than anything like the Holy Grail. Through these lifelines, the Lord of life comes to us in grace, in love, and in mercy. Oh, that all truly Gospel-centered congregations would sing, shout, and celebrate these fabulous facets of the Gospel! So many people are looking for the right things in all the wrong places. Rather than foundering in fickle feelings, we can point them to the place of God's grace—Word and sacrament.

PARAMOUNT

Correctly applying Law and Gospel in their families is of paramount importance for parents. Law and Gospel are more than just the two great teachings of the Bible. They are more than the Rosetta stone to unlock the message of scripture. They are the handles for parents to instruct and motivate their children and one another.

Earlier in the book, we alluded to the fact that the Law comprises those teachings that tell us what we should or should not do. They are the do's and the don'ts. They are freedom's footsteps for the Christian. But they are also "a mirror bright to bring the inbred sin to light," so that the Gospel can do its proper work. Eli failed to teach his sons the law, and they grew up like wild weeds and exploited everybody in sight.

The Gospel is the Good News of what God has done for us through His Son, Jesus Christ. It is the story of how Jesus died in our place to pay for our sins. Free salvation. Eternal life. Heaven. God is for you. Total absolution. Knowledge that you are loved. All of this is the Good News of the Gospel. Bear in mind that when the Hebrew Bible uses the word *Torah* for Law (Psalms 1:2), here we have a blessed exception to what we have just written. Here Law, or Torah, stands for God's Law and Gospel, what we must do, and what God has done to save us—guidelines and lifelines.

It is a lifelong art to learn how to apply Law and Gospel. None of us comes close. Yet, the better one becomes, the more one's family will have what it really needs.

THE TEACHER OF TEACHERS, THE PARENT OF PARENTS

Parents must learn by the Holy Spirit not to mete out the Law when their children are sorry for their sins. They must resist giving the Gospel to their children when they are smug and defiant. As they dispense God's Law and Gospel, it is imperative that they do it with humility and gentleness, treating others' faults as graciously as their own.

In his book, *The Proper Distinction between Law and Gospel*, C.F.W. Walther declared to preachers what the dominant note should be in their pulpit work. He wrote, "The Word of God is not rightly divided when the person teaching it does not allow the

Gospel to have a general predominance in his teaching." What Walther said to preachers applies to parents and spouses. Is the dominant note in your family, that little congregation where you live, the Law or the Gospel?

Too many parents and spouses could be described as "the accusative case." They nag. They complain. They are known, above all, for beleaguering their children with the Law; rather than being known for lifting them up by the Gospel. For every word of affirmation, they speak ten words of condemnation. They are Law-heavy and Gospel-light. Then they are shocked when their children run away and their spouse leaves them. Since the Law accuses, drives a person to despair, and kills, it will bring about no real improvement in the life of the battered individual. Only the Gospel heals and gives life.

THE CHIEF NOTE

Walther told pastors of his day it was "of *paramount* importance" for the Gospel to be the dominant note in their preaching. The Good News of Jesus alone produces the unselfish love people so inwardly crave. While one may not proclaim enough law in a family, you can never proclaim too much Gospel.

As much as anything, we need families who see the need of living under a roof where the Gospel is the chief note. When the Gospel is given little space, a home will be an unhappy place. When the Gospel is the dominant note, the lifelines of love will conduct into such a home impulses to carry out the guidelines of love.

FINALLY

Experts tell us that in recent years large numbers of television viewers have been on a "reality binge." These viewers seek out shows, programs, and movies that replay "live" rescue missions. In a subliminal search for meaning in life, these restless souls turn to the post mortem replay of these love and rescue stories.

The hunger of the "reality binge" seekers isn't new. A great African churchman sixteen centuries earlier "binged" upon a smorgasbord of earth-bound manna meals before finding satisfaction in the Bread of Life, Jesus Christ. In his *Confessions*, St. Augustine stated: "(O Lord) You stir man to take pleasure in praising you, because you have made us for yourself, and our heart is restless until it rests in you."

The goal of *The Lifelines of Love* has been to soothe the restless heart, to feed the hungry soul, to point people to the God of reality. For only when people are drawn close to the God of reality can they find strength to love. This God, who is passionately and profoundly involved in history, is not a distant deity. He is not the listless Hindu god, loveless Greek god, mute god of Taoism, nor the deadly diatribe god Allah. In the cataclysmic event of the cross, the God of reality has spoken. He is the God who has drawn near in the person and work of Jesus Christ.

There is a mystery, unity, and plurality in the God of reality. Though one in essence, this God alone has the powerful plurality of persons to qualify as the God of love; for love implies more than just one person. And what a love it is! From eternity, God the Father authors a love and rescue mission; in the fullness of time, God the Son serves as the cross-bearing agent of this mission; and today, through *The Lifelines of Love*—Word and Sacrament—the Holy Spirit pours out this love (Ephesians 1:3-14; Romans 5:5).

So many people are hungering for the right thing, but looking in all the wrong places. The task of the truly evangelical ministry is to point people to *The Lifelines of Love* that Messiah has ordained to put people in contact with the divine. The heaven-ordained oasis by which parched souls in this desert world become watered will ever remain holy baptism, holy absolution, Holy Communion, and the Holy Gospel rightly administered and correctly proclaimed. These are not only *The Lifelines of Love*, but the true fountains of life.

Recently a Christian couple shared with me a beautiful sketch of their tombstone they plan to have placed in our church cemetery. Engraved in banner form across the stone are the words "By Grace Are Ye Saved Through Faith" (Ephesians 2:8). Above these words is the surname of this *Lifelines of Love* couple. To the left of their last name will be a chiseled-in-the-stone picture of a baptismal shell and to the right a chiseled-in-the-stone picture of a Lord's Supper chalice. To their children as well as their children's children, they want to emphasize the importance of *The Lifelines of Love*. In addition, they want their posterity to know that not only is one saved by grace alone, but that this grace comes to us through the means of grace that Christ has appointed.

Over thirty-three years ago, I asked a brilliant but humble Christian professor the key to a strong faith and a close walk with the Lord. In simple words Dr. Walter Wente said, "Be around Word and Sacrament. Be around Word and Sacrament." I tucked those words in mind that day, little realizing at the time that this wise theologian had set my sights upon *The Lifelines of Love*. My prayer for all Christians who read this book is that they nestle Dr. Wente's words in their hearts and make them a motto for their homes.

PSALM ONE — A NEW TESTAMENT INTERPRETATION

Blessed is the man who does not follow the advice of wicked people, or takes the path of the unrepentant sinners, or joins the company of those who scoff at God's Word.

Rather his deep delight is God's Law and Gospel, and he mulls, muses, and meditates upon these teachings day and night!

He is like a sturdy cypress tree planted beside streams, a tree which yields abundant fruit continually and whose leaves do not wither, for they are watered by the Lifelines of Love!

Ultimately, he succeeds in everything he does.

Not so the unrepentant! They are like the chaff the wind blows away.

Therefore the wicked will not stand on Judgment Day;

Neither the unrepentant sinners,

But those who live from God's righteousness

Ah, they shall surely stand!

The Lord knows the way of those who believe in the Righteous One,

But the way of the wicked will be an eternal dead-end!

Family Prayers

Luther's Morning Prayer

I thank Thee, my Heavenly Father, through Jesus Christ, Thy dear Son, that Thou hast kept me this night from all harm and danger; and I pray Thee that Thou wouldst keep me this day also from sin and every evil, that all my doings and life may please Thee. For into Thy hands I commend myself, my body and soul, and all things. Let Thy holy angel be with me that the wicked Foe may have no power over me. Amen.

Luther's Evening Prayer

I thank Thee, my heavenly Father, through Jesus Christ, Thy dear Son, that Thou hast graciously kept me this day; and I pray Thee that Thou wouldst forgive me all my sins where I have done wrong, and graciously keep me this night. For into Thy hands I commend myself, body and soul, and all things. Let Thy holy angel be with me, that the wicked Foe may have no power over me. Amen.

Table Prayer

Come Lord Jesus, be our guest, and let these gifts to us be blessed. Amen.

Table Prayer For Tots

Thank You, Jesus, for our food. Amen.

Table Prayer For Children

Feed Thy children, God most holy, Comfort sinners poor and lowly; O Thou Bread of Life from heaven, Bless the food Thou here hast given! As these gifts the body nourish, May our souls in graces flourish Till with saints in heav'nly splendor, At Thy feast due thanks we render.
Amen.
—Johann Heermann, 1656 TLH 659, LW 468

Study Notes

Pastor Todd R. Jerabek

Pre-1   What are some differences between men and women?

Pre-2   Communication is important in marriage.

List those things about which you need to have good lines of communication.

Pre-3   According to Pastor Kurowski, what are the "Lifelines" of love?

QUESTIONS

CHAPTER 1 – FOUNDATION

1. John and Mary were wed for only seven months before their marriage was in trouble. What was missing from their marriage?

   _____

   _____

   _____

   _____

2. What is the one thing they need for their marriage?

   _____

   _____

   _____

   _____

3.   We can visibly see the faults in others; do we see them in ourselves?

_____

_____

_____

4.   We all have a destructive spirit as our inheritance from our first parents, Adam and Eve. What is that spirit?

_____

_____

_____

5.   What is the cure to "self-justification"?

_____

_____

_____

6.   What do people need to know before the love of God can free them from their sins?

_____

_____

_____

7.   What are the channels through which God gives us power for our life here, the power to love others?

_____

_____

_____

8. What can stand in the way of this power from God?

_____

_____

_____

9. What is wrong with trying to follow "guidelines" (the Law) for marriage?

_____

_____

_____

10. Where does God give to His people the "Lifelines of Love"? Name them:

_____

_____

_____

11. Can a spouse be the source of living happily ever after?

_____

_____

_____

12. The deepest joy in life comes from what?

_____

_____

_____

_____

Chapter 2 – Forgiveness

1. What is the most powerful therapeutic remedy in the world?

   _____

   _____

   _____

   _____

2. A. How does God give to us this medicine of forgiveness?

   _____

   _____

   _____

   _____

   B. Where do we receive these things as God comes to us?

   _____

   _____

   _____

   _____

3. As we receive forgiveness, it also builds two things, the bonds that bind couples together. What are these two things?

   _____

   _____

   _____

4.   Why is it very easy to remember the Law and point out
      the wrong things?

      _____

      _____

      _____

      _____

5.   When you stand at the foot of the cross and see all that
      Christ has done for you, when you sit back and contem-
      plate all the sins you have committed, and that for them
      Christ died, it moves you to do what to others?

      _____

      _____

      _____

      _____

6.   When someone sins against us, it is difficult to put that
      in the past and forget about it. There is, however, a way
      to begin the healing and to move forward. This healing
      comes from an outside source. How do you receive it?

      _____

      _____

      _____

      _____

7.   What are the means by which it is dispensed?

      _____

      _____

      _____

8. Our hearts need the assurance of forgiveness on a regular basis. Forgiving does not equal forgetting, nor is forgetting a requirement for the giving of forgiveness. Forgiveness is a 100 percent free gift. When it talks about God forgetting our sins, it doesn't mean that it is forgotten, for God knows all things. What then, does it mean?

    _____

    _____

    _____

    _____

9. When we are forgiven, we are moved to forgive others. When we realize and know in our hearts how much God puts up with on our account, we are given the power of forbearance to put up with the faults of others. Should you expect perfection, or near perfection, in a spouse?

    _____

    _____

    _____

    _____

10. Each partner in a marriage is what? (See Romans 3:10-20)

    _____

    _____

    _____

    _____

11. Sin is a "spitting in God's eye" thing. That means it is not a minor matter. In fact, what we would consider the most inoffensive and harmless of sins, God considers eternally damning. After all, "the wages of sin," any kind of sin, no matter how seemingly harmless, "is death." When we look at our own individual sinfulness, it will keep us humble. Yet, what has God done with *all* of our sins?

_____

_____

_____

_____

12. Take time to read the account of Jesus and the sinful woman in Luke 7:36-50.

_____

_____

_____

_____

A. What is wrong with this woman?

_____

_____

_____

B. Yet Jesus declared her what?

_____

_____

_____

C. By declaring to her forgiveness, Jesus places her in a right relationship with God. And because of the *great* amount of sins forgiven her, her love was equally *great*. Where forgiveness is felt very little, the love is equally very little. God creates faith in love through the forgiveness He gives. How great is your need for forgiveness?

_____

_____

_____

_____

13. The gift of forgiveness comes through the Church. What is the awesome event towering behind this gift?

_____

_____

_____

_____

14. When forgiveness is given, what other gifts of heaven are connected with it?

_____

_____

_____

_____

15. God's gift of forgiveness gives all these gifts. Is it important that we are embraced by the gift of forgiveness? How often?

_____

_____

_____

_____

16. Daily repentance drowns the Old Adam and brings to the surface the New Adam. What is the nature of this New Adam?

_____

_____

_____

_____

17. Love means "never having to say you're sorry," or so some people would have us believe. However, if spouses are short on saying "I am sorry" to God, they will find it equally hard to say "I'm sorry" to whom else?

_____

_____

_____

_____

Chapter 3 – Faith

1. Whenever there are broken promises or broken wedding vows, what else has failed?

   _____

   _____

   _____

   _____

2. Where faith in Christ flourishes, what flows forth?

   _____

   _____

   _____

   _____

3. List three Bible passages in which faith and love are mentioned together.

   _____

   _____

   _____

   _____

4. What is it that creates faith?

   _____

   _____

   _____

   _____

5. Too often our love is conditional. If you are pretty, I will love you. As long as you are you, I will love you. *Agape* love is what kind of love?

    _____

    _____

    _____

    _____

6. Jesus' death on the cross is important. What is just as important as His death?

    _____

    _____

    _____

    _____

7. Jesus gives an example of perfect love. Jesus gave His life for us, while we hated Him and sinned against Him. What ought we to do out of love for our brothers?

    _____

    _____

    _____

    _____

8. Note the sequence of events. First God's love comes to us, then we can love. To have the power to love, we must know what?

    _____

    _____

    _____

9. Just as a body needs nourishment to survive and grow, so
    does faith. Faith is built and nourished through "means"
    that God gives. Then the spouse, nourished by these
    "means," can cherish, forgive, and love the other. What
    are these realities that God uses to come to us and nourish
    us?

    _____

    _____

    _____

    _____

10. Where does God come and give these realities to
    people?

    _____

    _____

    _____

    _____

11. Daily sin grown in us; it needs to be controlled. Paul tells
    how to control sin. Like a beard needs daily clipping, what
    is the clipper that God uses daily to work in us love and
    forgiveness?

    _____

    _____

    _____

    _____

12. The Lord's Supper is a meal that "demands only hungry souls," souls that hunger to be loved by the grace of God. It is a meal that gives us what?

_____

_____

_____

_____

13. What is *agape's* path? (See also cute little cartoon)

_____

_____

_____

_____

CHAPTER 4 – FIDELITY

1. After David's fall into lust and temptation, he then had to cover his sin with murder. That one night of infidelity stained the rest of King David's life. Infidelity was a thief that robbed him of what?

   _____

   _____

   _____

   _____

2. In case of infidelity on the part of one spouse, is it all the responsibility of the one spouse that he or she strayed? Explain:

   _____

   _____

   _____

   _____

3. What is the refreshing news of a lifeline that will keep infidelity away and make fidelity and faithfulness a part of our lives?

   _____

   _____

   _____

   _____

4. What is the first component of a high-fidelity marriage?
    Read Chapters Four and Five each day between now and
    when we next meet.
    From Ephesians 4:32, what are some components of a
    strong friendship?

    _____

    _____

    _____

    _____

5. How do kindness and tenderheartedness come to us?

    _____

    _____

    _____

    _____

6. Intimacy is essential for a good, strong marriage. What is
    one of the main ingredients for intimacy?

    _____

    _____

    _____

    _____

7. Fear is one thing that breaks down communication. What
    causes fear to flee?

    _____

    _____

    _____

    _____

8.   Is there such a thing as a "good" fight?

_____

_____

_____

_____

9.   What happens that makes it good?

_____

_____

_____

_____

10. Can intimacy be overbearing? What can help?

_____

_____

_____

_____

11. A marriage is a lifelong commitment. Dietrich Bonhoeffer had a nice quote that emphasizes commitment as the glue to a marriage, not the feeling of love. Write the quote here.

_____

_____

_____

_____

12. With this attitude, is divorce ever an option? Think about that now. Do not come to the pastor later, saying, "We just don't love each other anymore." If that happens, then it is time for the pastor to say, "Well then, it is about time you started learning how to do so. Divorce is not an option."

_____

_____

_____

_____

13. A relationship needs to be built on feelings, or something else. What?

_____

_____

_____

_____

14. The marriage is also something that takes place in the bedroom. Describe what lovemaking should be to a couple?

_____

_____

_____

15. Hard work is needed to make a marriage wholesome and long lasting. What are some things that you can work on to make sure your marriage remains a high-fidelity marriage?

_____

_____

_____

16. A. What is the most important expert help and inspiration for your marriage? From where do these come?

_____

_____

_____

B. Where does this mean we should be on a *weekly* basis to maintain a healthy and strong marriage?

_____

_____

_____

17. A. Where is the battle for temptation lost—in the bed or the mind?

_____

_____

_____

B. What is the way to win this battle?

_____

_____

_____

18. A. Isolation is not a way to avoid temptation. What is the way to conquer temptation?

_____

_____

_____

QUESTIONS

B. We need to be fed what to have healthy love and life?

_____

_____

_____

19. A. Where does the ultimate affirmation of love take place?

_____

_____

_____

B. Explain how Jesus will be the "Yes" in your marriage.

_____

_____

_____

C. How do you work toward making the Gospel the dominant note of your marriage?

_____

_____

_____

Chapter 5 – Freedom

1. Ephesians 5:21-33 contains some of the most beautiful verses of God's Scriptures to husbands and wives. Men and women both misunderstand this portion of Scripture. Without reading further in Pastor Kurowski's book, read this passage from the New Testament and write what you think this message from God means.

   _____

   _____

   _____

   _____

2. Explain Matthew Henry's commentary in your own words.

   _____

   _____

   _____

   _____

3. When we as sinners look at God's Word, we look for all the loopholes. We want to be obedient to God, but we want to do it on our own terms, so we look for ways to interpret scripture for our benefit. What are the two major loopholes people invent when it comes to the order God has designed for the family?

   _____

   _____

   _____

   _____

4. What are the three models to which spouses submit? Circle the unique Christian model.

    _____

    _____

    _____

5. Explain God's plan of equality between men and women.

    _____

    _____

    _____

6. A. What are some of the ways people today disobey God in His established sexual orders?

    _____

    _____

    _____

    B. And what are the consequences of disobedience?

    _____

    _____

    _____

7. A. Jesus shows us about submission. Is submission an action that comes from the person who is submitting? Or is submission a ruling over by the one with more power?

    _____

    _____

    _____

THE LIFELINES OF LOVE

B. How did Jesus show submission?

_____

_____

_____

_____

C. Does the word "submission" suggest inferiority?

_____

_____

_____

_____

8. A. Dr. Kurowski describes a win-win situation in marriage. When both husband and wife submit to the Gospel of Christ, and the call to total servanthood to one another, both win. Give examples of how the situation becomes a losing situation.

_____

_____

_____

_____

B. Notice that within the Trinity there is a constant effort to give authority away to the other. Why is there no struggle for power within the Trinity?

_____

_____

_____

_____

9. What is the mindset St. Paul writes about which will deepen the oneness between husband and wife?

_____

_____

_____

_____

10. How can the husband's headship become perverted, a gross misuse of God's intended way it should happen?

_____

_____

_____

_____

11. A. What is love?

_____

_____

_____

_____

B. Matthew 20:26 shows where greatness comes from. From where?

_____

_____

_____

_____

12. Show how love, subjection (submission or subordination) and freedom are intimately tied together.

_____

_____

_____

_____

13. A. According to Martin Luther, what is the key connection between freedom and subjection?

_____

_____

_____

_____

    B. How does service fit into freedom?

_____

_____

_____

_____

14. The cross of Christ produces a spirit that subordinates itself to the will and word of God. How do you hope to make this work in your marriage?

_____

_____

_____

_____

CHAPTER 6 – FINANCES

1. Summarize the "world" philosophy about money.

   _____

   _____

   _____

   _____

2. Even though the "world" view of money is one thing, what does God's Word say about it through Solomon, one of the richest men ever?

   _____

   _____

   _____

   _____

3. What is Christ-esteem?

   _____

   _____

   _____

   _____

4. A. How much do you own? How much are you given of which you are to be a steward or manager?

   _____

   _____

   _____

B. What we have should be used for what purpose?

_____

_____

_____

5. What are the three things that should govern our outlook upon everything that happens to us? C.S. Lewis has another way of saying the same thing. What does he say?

_____

_____

_____

6. A. What is our first goal?

_____

_____

_____

B. The primary thing for which we should search? Where is this done?

_____

_____

_____

7. A. What should be our first priority so that we do not "chase" after the wind?

_____

_____

_____

B. The foremost purpose of God's Word is what?

_____

_____

_____

C. He also desires us to be what?

_____

_____

_____

8. What are the three "S's" of managing God's money? Explain them.

_____

_____

_____

9. A. What can we do to get God's assistance to help us with our financial concerns? Where is this found?

_____

_____

_____

B. How often should we use this tool God gives to us?

_____

_____

_____

10. A. What can you do to set goals and limits?

_____

_____

_____

B. What are the beginnings of a budget?

_____

_____

_____

C. How soon will you be able to have it all?

_____

_____

_____

11. A. What should you give back to God? How much should you give to the Lord's work?

_____

_____

_____

B. Good givers are usually liberal in giving what to Whom?

_____

_____

_____

12. A. Give some examples of good debt.

_____

_____

_____

B. Give some examples of bad debt.

_____

_____

_____

13. A. God calls us back to the lifelines; they are the treasures of heaven. What are they?

_____

_____

_____

B. Seek what? And what will be added unto you?

_____

_____

_____

_____

A Short Method to Help Create a Working Budget

List Assets

_____

_____

_____

List Debts
   A. Required Monthly

_____

_____

_____

List Assets
   B. Goals & Savings

_____

_____

_____

_____

CHAPTER 7 – FAMILY

1.   Upon what does the strength of a society stand or fall? What do people seek to find through this institution?

_____

_____

_____

2.   Why is there pain in families? What is the cause?

_____

_____

_____

3.   List the three models for parenting and describe each.

_____

_____

_____

4.   A. Who is it that teaches children the most?

_____

_____

_____

B.   What gives parents the power to be the best examples to their children that they can be?

_____

_____

_____

5. A. If children do not get family at home, they will go elsewhere to be part of "family." Where might that be?

    _____

    _____

    _____

    _____

    B. Why is society faltering, while families are failing?

    _____

    _____

    _____

6. Praise is an important part of parenting that may be often overlooked. What do we need to do to begin to praise?

    _____

    _____

    _____

7. A. Do love and discipline go together? Explain.

    _____

    _____

    _____

    B. Define the parameters of loving discipline.

    _____

    _____

    _____

    _____

8. A. What are the four arms of a well-balanced life?

_____

_____

_____

_____

    B. How does prayer fit in?

_____

_____

_____

    C. Give two examples of times to pray, and an acceptable prayer.

_____

_____

_____

9. A. How can we carry one another's burdens?

_____

_____

_____

    B. What is the prime procedure for coping with pressure?

_____

_____

_____

C. If this is true, where should we be every week?

_____

_____

_____

_____

10. What is the great glue to a strong family? Where do we receive this glue?

_____

_____

_____

_____

11. What three words need to be said regularly to each other and to the kids? Where do we get the supply to say these words to one another?

_____

_____

_____

_____

12. Patterns or traditions are important. Without traditions our lives fall apart. What are some traditions that you each have in your own families?

_____

_____

_____

_____

At mealtime:

Easter:

Ascension:

Pentecost:

Mother's Day:

Father's Day:

Fourth of July:

Thanksgiving:

Advent:

Christmas:

New Year's Eve:

At other times:

13. A. Define both Law and Gospel. Which should dominate?

_____

_____

_____

_____

   B. What are the Lifelines of Love?
       Finally, what is the key to a strong faith and close walk with the Lord?

_____

_____

_____

_____

CPSIA information can be obtained at www.ICGtesting.com
Printed in the USA
BVOW022204240412

288583BV00001B/6/A

9 781414 106878